MAD SCIENCE IN IMPERIAL CITY

FUTUREPOEM BOOKS
NEW YORK CITY
2005

MAD SCIENCE IN IMPERIAL CITY

SHANXING WANG

ISBN: 0-9716800-5-1

FIRST EDITION | FIRST PRINTING

This edition first published in paperback by Futurepoem books
Futurepoem books, P.O. Box 34, New York, NY 10014
www.futurepoem.com
Press Editor: Dan Machlin
Book Co-editor: Kristin Prevallet
2003/2004 Guest Editors: Edwin Torres, Heather Ramsdell, Kristin Prevallet

Design: Anthony Monahan (am@anthonymonahan.com)

Cover Images: Empire State Building © Anthony Monahan;
Terracotta Warriors and Tiananmen Square © Getty Images

Interior flap illustration © Anthony Monahan

Altered image of definition of "Abstract," on p. 27 originally from *American Heritage Dictionary of the English Language*. 4th ed. Boston: Houghton Mifflin, 2000.

Quote, p. 2, Gérard de Nerval, "*Les Chimères*" from Duncan, Robert. *Bending the Bow*. New York: New Directions, 1968, p. 92.

Quotes, p. 23, from Riemann, Bernhard. Trans. by William Kingdon Clifford. "On the Hypotheses Which Lie at the Bases of Geometry." *Nature*, Vol. VIII. Nos. 183, 184, pp. 14-17, 36, 27; Gell-Mann, Murry. *The Quark and the Jaguar: Adventures in the Simple and Complex*. New York: Owl Books, 1994, p. 180.

Quote, p. 112, Handke, Peter. *Kaspar and Other Plays*. Trans. by Michael Roloff. New York: Hill and Wang, 1989, p. 86.

Text set in Scala and Computer Modern.
Printed in the United States of America on acid-free paper.

This book was made possible, in part, by grants from the New York State Council on the Arts Literature Program, a state agency, Fractured Atlas, the New York Community Trust, and the Fund for Poetry. Futurepoem receives non-profit sponsorship for grants and donations through NYSCA Fractured Atlas Productions, Inc., a non-profit 501(c)3 organization.

Distributed to the trade by Small Press Distribution, Berkeley, California
Toll-free number (U.S. only): 800.869.7553
Bay area/International: 510.524.1668
orders@spdbooks.org
www.spdbooks.org

This text issues forth from and now returns to all who have influenced me along the way—whose names are too numerous to list in this small space. However too late and immaterial it is, this book has always been intended to appeal to my parents, to forgive my ignorance, willfulness, and total failure to perform my given role. I am indebted to my sisters and brothers, Phoebe & Shawn, Haixin, Hexin & Bao, Chuanxin & Janet. I've been most consistently challenged and sustained by Hexin, a precocious poet herself, by her poems and our literary conversations. This book is an outgrowth of seeds largely planted in workshops I attended from fall 2001 to summer 2003 at Rutgers, the Poetry Project, and Naropa University. My chronological thanks go to Sabrina Orah Mark, Catherine Texier, Anne Waldman, Renee Gladman, Kristin Prevallet, Phyllis Wat, Evelyn Reilly, Lewis Warsh, David Henderson, Lisa Birman, Barrett Watten, Eleni Sikelianos, Mark Jensen, Reed Bye, and Jena Osman, for encouragements or critiques at different points. An earlier version of "A's Degeneracy" appeared in the Naropa *Summer Writing Program 2003 Magazine*. Thanks to Kristin Palm, the poetry editor of *580 Split* (#6), for using "J Integral," and to Monica de la Torre, the poetry editor of *The Brooklyn Rail*, for publishing "Probes of Near-Field Optical Microscopy," and two excerpts from "A's Degeneracy." I am grateful to Eleni Sikelianos for pointing me to Futurepoem Books. Thanks to Marcella Durand for her careful proofreading. Thanks to Anthony Monahan for his great cover design. I am most thankful to the 2003-04 editors of Futurepoem Books, Edwin Torres, Kristen Prevallet, Heather Ramsdell and Dan Machlin, and to Kristin and Dan in particular, for their editorial insights, care and infinite patience in shaping the book into its final form.

CONTENTS

PVD   1

PROBES OF NEAR-FIELD OPTICAL MICROSCOPY

J INTEGRAL   17

A's DEGENERACY   23

HOW TO WRITE · HOW WRITE TO · TO HOW WRITE · TO WRITE
HOW · WRITE HOW TO · WRITE TO HOW · HOW TO WRITE HOW ·
HOW WRITE TO HOW · TO HOW WRITE TO · TO WRITE HOW TO ·
WRITE HOW TO WRITE · WRITE TO HOW WRITE · HOW TO WRITE
TO · HOW WRITE TO TO · TO HOW WRITE WRITE · TO WRITE
HOW WRITE · WRITE HOW TO HOW · WRITE TO HOW HOW ·
HOW TO WRITE WRITE · HOW WRITE TO WRITE · TO HOW WRITE
HOW · TO WRITE HOW HOW · WRITE HOW TO TO · WRITE TO
HOW TO · HOW TO WRITE HOW TO

T SQUARE   111

FROM ANGULARITY IN NOTE G

A mystery of love lies concealed in the metal;

'everything is sentient!'

—Gérard de Nerval, "*Les Chimères*"
  (Translated by Robert Duncan)

Counterclockwise it starts to turn. My turn. So I begin. But I am at a loss to utter.

I search in the audience but the assuring face is nowhere. But still. I take deep breaths like in the retreat to steady my stuttering, to recover the loss of lines of utterance.

Once again I begin. This is from *Terracotta Warriors Quartet*, the beginning of which still escapes me. *Louder.* I can't speak any louder. Inertia runs its due course. Stone and dream. I continue mumbling. Passages from page one, the synopsis. Instead I have my conference paper *Nanoscale Prototyping of Anthropoid Integrated Circuits.* Where did I place/misplace the manuscript?

After rapid dry run it pauses its rotation. As if taking another deep breath. I ease into the 2nd quadrant of the circular hall. It turns into a music stage. I turn to the 2nd page. Literature review and introduction. From the statistical ensemble of string instruments, his violin sings his magic words.

I ask the faceless him if he still plays the demonic Paganini. He says he's been rehearsing and recorded all 15 string quartets by Shostakovich (whom he loves more than any other composer) with his new band *From the Mausoleum*. He asks me if we can again subject ourselves to the direct current of music in the cramped dorm room, with all lights off, as we always did. If only he were . . . I sigh.

Across River Y that pours down from heavenly sky, every early July we boarded the train home from the ancient city; midway I changed to another while he continued on to the capital.

But the music never discontinued. I am the standing waves confined in the delicate metal strings of his violin, the tensions and therefore frequencies of the notes which are measured by four characteristic levels, *Aut, Win, Spr, Sum*, respectively, according to the seasons in the ancient city. It follows from well-established fact that elastic material undergoes thermal expansion or contraction when temperature fluctuates.

He insists we watch *The Great Escape*. For the 13th time. I almost laugh. What a great comedy. Not hearing me, his voice disappears.

It resumes spinning. At even slower speed. Burdened by the solidification and densification of its own memory and the difficulty of telling it faithfully.

Your shaven head, out of the blue, out of the magnificent yellow robe, struts towards me, your eyes fixed on papers in my left hand, as if asking what crap they are. Did you, can you read my last letters, what's the point of my writing if you don't, can't read them.

Yes, it is music. It is classical music. Not classical mechanics. Slicing the muddy water at the estuary of River Y, staring into the distant ocean, you said, Across it's a wonderland. *From the New World* was your favorite symphony. You played it in the smoky beach bar.

You pass by me without saying a word, as if you didn't see me, or saw me but could not make out the thick masked face, or recognized it but didn't hear a thing or heard me but couldn't apprehend anything and therefore resented my muteness or my terribly altered accent, or understood my every word but simply didn't want to talk to me, because I haven't written you since sending you the musical Xmas card, because I didn't visit, most disturbingly, because the thought of visiting you never occurred to me until this writing—it really never happened if you can't write about it, even once, even after learning about your readmission into the institution, even at this very moment of reading, as if I had been and were still being terrified by the possibility of being *there* again, of being held *there* for life.

You keep walking, along the dotted straight line, through the thick wall and out of the hall.

It has halted again. The 3rd quadrant greets me. I am in the 3rd page. The experimental set-up and procedures. It is an elevated Ping-Pong court. You stare at me across the blue *Butterfly* table.

We battle the 38 mm white *Double Happiness* Ping-Pong ball for each point, with our *Friendship* rackets, while he sits at the net flipping the scoreboard. You hop to the left corner of your side of the table, turn the torso to the right and swing the racket backwards. You push the right leg upwards, in a twist turn the torso to the left. With your wrist snapping, the accelerating racket, the extension of your right arm hits the incoming ball. It bounces off the sweet spot of the racket into the air, flies along a perfect parabola barely clearing the net, lands near the net on the far-left corner of my side of the table, then bounces off again, curves away from the table farther to my left and falls onto the floor, still spinning hissingly. I missed the ball completely. I lose the game again. Lose three games straight. But I had you, and all the air you carried around you.

Afterwards, I lost myself again in the hot tub steam.

The applause erupts. For the step-around inside-out forehand loop? My breath rate triples to compensate for the rapid depletion of oxygen in my chest. As if I were climbing a steep mountain. Where did I lose my story?

You pull me up along the rocky road to the temple, like on the 12 km long winding path leading to the top of Mountain H. In our 1st spring excursion, you accompanied me all the way up and down the single-path slope. Even though 20 other names separate us in the class roster. On the summit you poured spring water into my mouth, as he took a snapshot. A deep imprint in the thin film of my memory. You raised questions about the location, shape, velocity, and temperature of the clouds, while we were waiting for the sunrise, shivering in the wind.

Snow was not imaginary in April. On the summit. The thin air. It spins again.

When you 1st addressed me in the ancient city of terracotta warriors, *Du Lu Ji Ba Ge So*, I replied, *E Shi Ji Qian*, uttering utterly different dialects of the southern and northern intonation, and neither of us understood a word the other said, causing others around us (including him) to burst out laughing. But we were immediately drawn to each other when we found out our birthdays were hours apart.

Since then I've never uttered another sentence in my native dialect. Since then I've been speaking pidgin mandarin.

My mandarin, accented by your southern tone. *Lian yu jiao zi ba jian duei; jian duei jiao zi ba lian yu*, or *continuity is that which is not interrupted; interruption is that which is not continuous*, as I recited Prof. Z's circular remarks before he introduced rigorous definitions.

On the other hand, it is he who was obsessed with dialects, even with the much-coveted standard mandarin tongue, his native tongue inherited from the last dynasty and toned by the new empire misnamed as republic, in the same capital. He subscribed to *Geographical Names & Vernaculars*. To mimic the juicy dialogues between the witty orchestra conductor and the clumsy plumber, we went to watch *The Great Escape* 12 times, 3 times in a day.

He was a natural voice imitator. He raved at me *Four Quartets*. Sitting next to each other in the last row of the packed classroom, we took turns writing down lines of

Didi and *Gogo* in my forever new class notebook. We waited and waited. But nothing happened. Until.

It stops again and I look into the 4th quadrant. My last page. Theoretical modeling. It becomes a chessboard.

Grinning he moves his red Knight toward my black Guard. After long deliberation I reposition my black Cannon behind his red Elephant.

All our Soldiers are martyred after fording River C. All our petitions were dismissed as abracadabra, and then denounced as anti-spin.

The lost cause. The lost case. What's the cause of the lost case? What's the case of the lost cause? What is the absent *utopia* in the cause of the case? Who is this strange *you* in the case of the cause? Doesn't make any sense.

I fumbled my way in the glowing boulevard of diction; I was brutalized by policemen *wu zhuang dao ya chi* (armed to teeth) in the dark alleys of syntax. In the new world of words, a worn ballpoint released by terracotta warriors traveling over earthy maps with English legends, targeting the demons of June.

I forget everything. I forgive nothing.

Above all I forgive not myself, not my powerlessness and cowardice, not my silence and absence in all these years.

Both Kings have fallen into sound sleep. Bored by our fruitless ruminations and dumb maneuvers. So our promise to exchange moves across the ocean by letters, one move each month.

Words exhaust themselves at unbelievable speed. Is it due to their innate infertility, or the immense river of voids, which devours all words rushing out of mouths before they ever make it to the other bank of ears, or the fact that there exist too many words that we are too afraid to utter, in order not to be hurt or hurt?

I've been misled by contexts or contents or discontents or contentions, formats or forms or pre-forms or uniforms of love. I've been possessed by desires. My desires without legitimate names. I am sweating.

You declare the game is a draw. I am wide awake again.

To write is the most decisive move to break the draw.

I raise my head from the chessboard for another breath. In the wall mirror appears a white statue, a she-he. Who must have been behind, or in front of, or beside me, watching and listening to me attentively all this time.

Mechanical chatters stream in. The air dies off. It revolves with abandon.

I am being sucked into a rapidly revolving heat sink. I look up to locate the sun. Two entwined nudes stand still in the ceiling mirror. One says, My life—a loaded gun; another, Emily, clicking metallic.

Is the 1st voice that of Emily Dickinson? But Emily has been dead for more than a centenary. Yet stranger things had happened in the capital.

The other voice resembling hers asks me who the person under me is. I instantly slide off the body and onto the marble floor. The heat is quickly conducted away.

I look to my left, you prostrate and erect in repetitions, as if stretching to warm up for a new game; I look to my right, he kneeling down wags the tongue, as if having switched from string to wind instrument.

In unison you beg, Sunflower, open the gate, please.

It is such a singular security between the ordered pair.

I look at the body; she-he is breathless, almost of human size. Another closer look reveals curves of the statue.

To locate the Cartesian origin and to feel the surface texture of true love, I'd make love to a stone.

Fireworks explode like thunderbolts, followed by an army of bulldozers, which rolls amuck. Watch out, barbarians are coming, I cry. I don't hear an echo.

It screeches to rest. With a cursory *thank you* I end the reading without summary, without conclusion. I toss my pages into the air. I am back to my unknown starting position; I am back to the 1st quadrant of the chaotic hall.

All mirrors are gone. Both she and Emily have vanished. Vapors circulate, bluish gray, like tear gas smoke.

The audience stands up and everyone nibbles their neighbor's ear, as if another revolution were fermenting.

I was wrong. There're no barbarians at all.

Revolution, a revolving illusion about a virtual axis.

It was covered by a huge transparent bell jar within the hall. A red flag drooping on the long steel spindle in the center, looking down on the scattered pages.

I am the test subject for a new experiment of PVD (Physical Voice Deposition) onto the marble stage. It is the rotary mechanical pump and multistage diffusion pump located somewhere outside the hall that have been chattering to attain the ultrahigh vacuum indispensable for the deposition process.

But the vacuumed bell jar couldn't withstand the atmospheric pressure. The vacuumed bell jar collapsed under uniformly distributed external pressure.

The gaseous suspension of particles, the voice particles. Are they produced by vaporization of or through impact by high-energy foreign ions on parts of speech in my utterance? What and where are the energy sources?

In the limelight, she-he reads in a familiar tone but strange patois, her-his chest vibrating with extraordinary verbal energy. Side by side, her body following her-his rise and fall, she translates her-his lines verbatim. Slender as a willow, dark as charcoal, he, holding the ground to her-his right, plays *Meditation* with the old violin, while you pace to and fro on her left, with unsteady steps in irregular patterns, murmuring *I don't know what.*

I am at a loss to understand why marble is sexier than she, he, she-he, it, you, and I.

With the stage stay abused pages. All my characters have escaped the massacre via lost pages, partying for their sudden liberation in the turbulent air.

The pumps rattle like barbarians, vacuuming the entire hall into a super bell jar. The audience is all gone. So are she, he, she-he, and you. Only ghost lights illuminate the hollow, reflected repeatedly from the interior surface of the luxuriantly lit hall. Or the bell jar of my cylindrically bloated skull?

It turns again, clockwise, its renewed determination defying any doubt about or attempt to reverse the direction of motion.

Speechless, I stand alone on the rotating stage, like a giant Ping-Pong ball glued onto the marble table, spinning and spinning, about an axis not of its own, while you are at peace in the other world, in the world of others. Are you? Where are you?

The tenuous air carries the crystalline voice:

Marble goddess, cracking of your naked

smooth ionic chest beneath parading mass,

sang our secret song of fusion fancied,

shaky in the dawn the brimstone fireballs.

I, the bronze-man, seared by raging flames,

held inside the aging mold of rusty

steel alloyed with tungsten liars, lead traps,

yanked my metallic ears, for poetry.

Your broken chips refill my hungry mouth;

by trial-and-error, I am making love

to you anew, to find our bonding strength,

rebuffing what supreme computers give.

Suck up all my free electrons, plasm!

Press. Covalent diamond. Manic. Vacuum.

I am at a loss to identify whom and where this voice originates from and where it intends to rest.

A new voice recording experiment begins in this soundproof cylindrical hell.

But I am already getting tired of all this. I have nothing more to read.

I want just to listen, listen, listen.

Who is speaking?

Who is he talking about?

What guards?

Where were they?

Why were the dialogues so stiff?

Did they really challenge him about his name?

Is it AM or FM or PM or SM?

Did you sign your name?

How many times did you sign?

Was it in the triangle?

Can you show it without telling?

How does this advance your story?

Aren't the lists too static?

Aren't you trying too hard?

Did you go through a dictionary?

Did you go through a dictator?

Did the gate open?

Is there a plot?

Who were the masterminds behind it?

Must you twist your story to please prick heads and pussy stomach?

Is this happening before or after?

Is it him or her?

Is the gender switch by accident?

He didn't open his eyes or all was imagined?

How long was the line on the boulevard?

How did they break the cordon?

What's the rationale behind the line break?

What is the gist of the line?

Where is it going?

Why are the quotation marks missing?

Why are you against the editorial line?

Have you swallowed enough red-inked shits?

Are you in line with the center?

What's the real purpose of your strike?

How far do you plan to take this strike?

Can you imagine the consequences of the present tense?

How could we *what?*

Why have we come?

Why do we come only now?

Couldn't you see it coming?

Can't you see the bottom line?

Can we work together on it?

What do I mean?

Are you trying so hard to impress?

Why are they wasted?

Can a giant panda swear?

Can a giant panda talk about depleting forest?

Can a baby giant panda know about androgen?

Aren't they translated from an alien speech?

Is there any common denominator among different tongues?

Was he really screaming loud?

Was it internal uttering?

Can you tone it down?

Why are you so fond of the long sentence?

How long is a long sentence?

What sentence are you referring to?

What's the law dictating the sentence?

So he died?

Are the letters just placeholders?

What's the deal with Scandinavia?

Is this meant to refer to the geographical area?

Were there two statues in the Square?

Are D and S fictional characters?

How many times did you go?

Did you go there with others?

Did you go there from the east or the west?

Why did you run away?

What's the point of repetition?

What exactly happened?

Did you see the carnage?

Are you still shaking?

When did it start?

What was the song?

Did it rain?

Was it blue or yellow?

Where is the price tag of freedom?

Did you throw the bottles?

Did you throw the basins?

Have you turned in your films?

Have you learned your lessons?

Is the world all that is the bookcase?

Do you know how to hold your tongue?

Do you know where to stick your ass?

Do I have a case?

J INTEGRAL

Today I am sick of the abundance of *I* in my story, capitalized or not, because the voice of this *I*, in its futile effort to win its case by sheer numbers, is chaotic, impotent, equivocal, and contradictory. Instead I go to others' stories, to hunt the specter of the hidden form of my story, lurking in the hundred-year-old narrative forest of how to say *I*

I meet K on each page I read. We unite in words over and over. K and *I*. For example, *kith* and *kin*, *drink*, *pick*, *kiss*, *kink*, *kill*. You get the picture of the state of the affair. Together we are a given in every story. But X is a rare species, X always wears a dark mist on his face if he appears on the pages at all. As if from weariness after the long solitary journey across the alphabet table of, or mistrust of the words. I know X and *I* joined each other in no less words. Like *Xi'an*. Or *existence, matrix, climax, anxiety, exile, extinction, Quixote, sphinx*. X and *I* stand side by side in this contextless heap of words, 75% of the time. Very encouraging. Why can't we always show up together in stories? I turn the pages of my math books to look for him, solve for him

At 4:30 AM on Monday X phoned me that K had died unexpectedly while playing his violin in Stockholm. Two days later X fled the city too and secluded herself in a remote monastery

I say she when I say K, and he X, or vice versa, as if I am positive about which should be he and which should be she. But in my speech I hopelessly misuse *he* as *she*, and *she* as *he*. Because in my mother tongue both *she* and *he* are pronounced as *ta*, with identical syllable and intonation. Or I have always been confounded by the similarities and differences between *she* and *he*. From pure appearance, *she* is different from *he* only by a serpent-like letter *S*. So *she* is the *S*ed *he* and *he* is the un*S*ed *she*. S. The bond between *he* and *she*. The sine wavy suture sewing *he* and *she*. I ride the surging wave to catch our lost fish and wonder who is in the air and who is in the water, *she* or *he*. I glide in both air and water because their interface has no thickness

I write *S* down in various fonts on the margins of the pages, to fill the blank space of my story. And I find myself walking alone on the deserted, crooked, willowy pavement, which consists of five *S*-shaped segments of different lengths but smoothly connected at the ends, which circumscribes the quiet man-made lake in the park of the ancient city, and along which I walked every week with K and X, along which we talked about the names of the fish jumping out of the water. Those fish jumping 10 feet above the water. We were so fascinated by the jumping fish that time and again we wanted to become three big fish playing with the stagnant water and the air saturated with the fragrance of willows and dewy grasses

I stretch, compress, twist *S* into different proportions, as if holding a newly discovered character. And I recognize the symbol of the line integral along the curve *J* in the *K*-*X*-*I* space, $\int_J PdK + QdX + RdI$, which perfectly approximates the accumulation in my memory of our hundred-time walk. J is short for *Jiaotong* in my mother tongue, which literally translates into *traffic, communication,* and *transport.* J contracts from *January* to *June* quietly longing for the scribbled scrambled miraculous spring. J immediately succeeds the severely handicapped I en route to K and X. No matter by what route, clockwise or counterclockwise, no matter what analytical method I try, be it table of standard integrals, integration by substitution, series expansion, Simpson's rule, or Gaussian quadrature, no matter what software I use, be it Maple, Mathematica, or Matlab, no matter what programming language I use, be it Fortran, Basic, or C++, no matter how many times I carry out my calculation, this integral always gives me the same result, that is 1980. I realize it depends only on our coordinates in space and time, fixed in my bleak memory park, since the path-independence of this integral is guaranteed by the fact that the integrand is the total differential of the mysterious function *F*, and this lake of my memory is a simply connected domain and its water is never ruffled

The question of the validity of the hypotheses of geometry in the infinitely small is bound up with the question of the ground of the metric relations of space . . . we must seek the ground of its metric relations outside it, in binding forces which act upon it.

—Georg Friedrich Bernhard Riemann
 "On the Hypotheses Which Lie at the Bases of Geometry"

String theory is an attempt at a deeper description of nature by thinking of an elementary particle not as a little point but as a loop of vibrating string. One of the basic things about a string is that it can vibrate in many different shapes or forms, which gives music of its beauty.

—Edward Witten
 Interview on NOVA, PBS

In 1963, when I assigned the name "quark" to the fundamental constituents of the nucleon, I had the sound first, without the spelling, which could have been "kwork." Then, in one of my occasional perusals of Finnegans Wake, by James Joyce, I came across the word "quark" in the phrase "Three quarks for Muster Mark."

—Murray Gell-Mann
 The Quark and the Jaguar

A'S DEGENERACY

Poetry died first, except that a couple of short lines spreading

hands and feet squint at God.

Passion followed second. Aren't we the third?

—Hexin Wang, "Learn to Be Alone"
  (Translated from the Chinese by Shanxing Wang)

I said, It's in the head.

I say, It's the head.

Where is my head? It's rolling back and forth on the periodic table on the waterbed, to futilely avoid the sliced punched sun diffusing through the fogs and drizzles through the duct-taped windows through the half-open Venetian blinds, from north to south and south to north, losing and gaining electrons periodically, wrapped in her hands, after spinning with no pre-specified orientation on vibration-isolation tables, computer tables, Ping-Pong tables, drafting tables, timetables, truth tables, and the table of contents of the impossible story.

I say, Unbearable anxiety about my 1st reading since I was thrown out of the Poetry House.

Yes, I say. His obscure remarks on that little yellow note stuck on my 1st poem, You can use the word W . . . in your . . . Poetry is not for you, A. I was told that he was referring to relying on concrete images and metaphors and resisting abstraction in poetry. But I had many grudges against this blasphemous affair between the Deity of Poetry and earthly images and metaphors.

Yes, I say. This is what I found in my *American Heritage Dictionary* (4th Ed.) through the long summer evening.

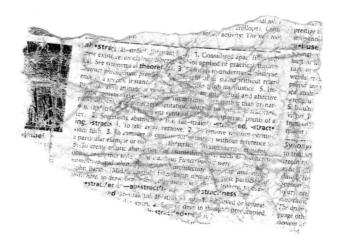

In the class-A clean room of the National Nanofabrication Laboratory in the heart of the Silicon Valley, under the ultrahigh-magnification AFM (Atomic Force Microscope), I thumbed through every page of the whole collection of poetry books stolen from the Public Library, and I found only dots, dotted straight lines, dotted arcs. Abstract geometrical entities banging my dilated eyeballs.

Yes, I say. Last night I had this dream. I the 3rd walk with my mother and the flock of my siblings, half-siblings, unknown siblings to a concert in the ball park named after an internet tycoon on the edge of the industrial park to hear old songs before her returning home across the ocean after a brief visit. I weep before the opaque wall of cacophony because I've suddenly noticed that she still looks incredibly young and beautiful and short after all these years she has lived through alone, because she has never been exposed to rock 'n' roll, let alone the name of the night's featured king of rock from that land. *A whore?* She squirms, making out a sluttish face. I never kissed the emperor on the face. I was never shown the face of my true father. She walks away alone saying nothing more. I wake. She never grows up and old. I have come up with a reasonable theory that her youth is the bio-logical consequence of her excessive cerebral drive and incessant promiscuous thought experiments. I had been wondering if she's the contorted persecuted but resilient mother of all the specters of *spiritual contamination.*

Yes, I say. While scribbling inside the biggest garbage can in the world, which is the rotten big apple, the deadly seductive big apple, a giant bowler atop his head, a physics dropout, a top quark that had escaped the confinement by the strong force inside the four-mile ring of Tevatron 30 miles west of Chicago and made its way all the way to the Times Square intact, with such an insanely long lifetime, bombarded my chemical-mechanically polished buttock in a pious tone, *You piece of digital shit, feel this heaviest poetic particle. Want a wild goose? Top quark,* a replacement for the original name *truth quark,* as if truth were never on the top poetic lists, was 1st observed in 1995 with a mass of 180 GeV after almost 20 years' relentless search. Once in a few billion collisions, physicists find the handwriting of top. We do not understand why tops are so massive. In fact the question still remains why anything has mass at all. From the garbage emerged two full-bottomed topless women, with $\frac{1}{3}$-empty glass bottles in the right hands, $\frac{1}{3}$-bitten apples in the left, blasting *son of a bitch* to my meticulously toned belly. As if the *bottom quark,* 1st named *beauty quark* and then rejected for its cuteness because beauty is not supposed to be found in the bottom, had traveled a visible distance before their further decay.

They broke in my every door. The B mesons and anti-B mesons. Again and again. The 3rd-generation poetic particles. They came as white jets inside the oval living room in my rented apartment among strangers, and for a picosecond yelled at me before their disappearance *ever a head* or *a line* or *a visible narrative thread,* like the omnipotent, omnipresent party phalluses wielded by invisible hands after the catastrophe.

Yes, I say. Every night they led me to poetry readings throughout the tiny village in the huge city; all I heard were *gramma, gamma, terma, truma, stigma, lemma, enigma, nema, acirema, lima, alma mater, Macarena, magma, magnolia, mahamaha.* All those *mas,* also signifying *horse* in my mother tongue, moaned fettered to the prefix *ma-* or suffix *-ma,* like ma's fainter and fainter begging at ever longer intervals across the ocean, *Will your over-educated and therefore overly curled-up hairs splice the strained hemp string of professional carnelian beads.* I x-ed out the vertical axes of 99 asterisks out of every 100 during and after all readings. I was unable to tell any stars with my defective glasses.

Live hyperbolic-spirally (about the axis of evil and approaching the asymptote why = a); write straight.

Throughout my triangular journey I wrote ma every other week to make up a story on my contribution to the latest progress in nanotechnology.

How did I miss my mother's tongue? How I miss my mother's tongue. How did I let it slip away? Yet never completely out of my view. Mother tongue, as mouthed by others around me outside motherland in the absence of ma, not the way ma spoke, not spoken by ma, terrifies me wherever I go. The more articulated, the more it adds to my existing fear.

Yes, I was, I say. With stacks of translated books on the 30,000 m^2 anvil inside a century-old case-hardened spur gear shaped in Germany. They came out of the shelves of the closet and howled like the Mediterranean tidal waves, with still-fresh winds and rains and frosts, even tens of thousands of miles away, even decades after their heydays. The French.

When was my golden moment?

Yes, I was, I say. Batons, bayonets, butterflies, blood everywhere.

Where did my golden moment go?

SHE: Would you let me comb your hair?

She bends towards me and snaps at my revolver with military precision. Trembling vice I've always been inculcated to stay away from. Take between the bleeding lip's dark make-up sheen, running alphabets, loaded rounds, unraveling, reveling. Once, twice, three times. Like in the song. A closed string winds around a compact dimension an integral number of times, which leads to winding modes of oscillation.

> *Dear S:*
>
> *Are you the skinny three-haired boy begging food for thought in the capital or the three snorts of the aphasic giant panda in the National Zoo?*

Yes, I was, I was, I say, as soon as her lower lip starts a barely discernible downward motion suggesting the question *were you stoned.* In the Bare Bar in the basement on the Telenet Ave I racked my brain with abstract and abstraction, my *American Heritage* under my elbow. I downed 10 glasses of AMF, pondering about the relationship between AMF and AFM, weighing each genre of MFA, drowning my poetic aspiration in fictitious horse urine with phosphorous smell. In the high chair of intoxicated spirit, I hailed *giant panda rights, read this,* to the austere Chief Justice drinking at the other end of the bar, tossed my oversized manuscript at shooters of dark rum in her loaded tray, and in less than a picosecond my fine analytic and ultrasensitive mind fled to Jupiter, *Motherfucker,* her voice the rubbing between sheets of gunmetal, and her words fragmentation grenades of legalized cowshit.

In the dim light I groped for Kant's pure reason and my silvered revolver . . .

SHE: Gun, the bastard son of God and nun, what a bitch.

Bitch or birch, is there any difference beyond a few incoherent sidekicks on the little heads and toes of the vertical trunk?

I kneaded, I rapped, I licked and lapped the trunk of the reticent birch tree in the open air, and blood instantly gushed from the fresh bruise on my palm and tongue as if to make up the lack of lubricating fluid, flooding me with questions about molecular mechanisms of sliding friction between dissimilar solid surfaces,

about the insanity of birch.

I must have mistaken birch for cherry. I must have mistaken the deciduous birch for bamboo shoot. I must have mistaken the robust birch facing the ivory cubicle for the flagpoles on the boulevard. I must have mistaken the hard-skinned birch outside the nanofabrication lab for the tender thigh of the marble statue. I must have mistaken the transplanted skew symmetric birch matrix greening the postmodern factory complex in the industrial park, the postmortem phalluses, for the lonesome withering willow meditating the nature of slow slaughtering by time at the man-made lake in the heart of the ancient city, the ancient thing, beneath which under the tired sun in our last spring together in the ancient city, I was suddenly surrounded by, or awakened to, without being awake without knowing without even trying to know without feeling any motion of the earth under me, for a seemingly indefinite period of time, but in fact maybe just a 30-second period or moment, after spending months to sort out freshly translated willow lines in the forest of Zarathustra, the harmonious oscillation of unknown golden flowers moving and unmoving at the same time, while she and he were perusing the cellular structures of fallen cherry petals and debating the validity of my cubic spline interpolation model on the functional dependence between *2nd sex* and *1st love* in the east or west garden, as the day was trotting on the numb asphalt main road, on the worn red-brick sidewalks, on the polished paving stones of the winding path around the lake, on my anxiety tromping, on our parting day galloping in anticipation of the restless railways that split at the edge of the ancient city and zigzag their separate ways, one eastbound but slightly southwards to the coast, another along the diagonal dividing east and north to the capital, and then I lost it forever the moment I awoke, the moment I reopened my sore eyes to the children, mothers, trees, birds, chatters, and vapors over the lake revolving relentlessly around me, the moment I strived to reregister the harmonic of the swing.

> *Dear S:*
>
> *My sincere apologia for my failure of getting up again in the morning*
> *I tried did try and couldn't but I have finally got the magic pill without*
> *a bill.*

There is no native friend beyond the Pass, I toasted tears to K and X respectively in our last partings at the ancient train station, where for the 1st time I was really born on the shining day in early September, that is, puffed from the singing mouth of my suddenly jubilant ma over a very long distance, over cities, rivers, mountains, and the sweeping field of fertility.

While she boarded the train to and was lost in the capital to explore new dimensions in the October sky, and he the bustling coastal city S to trace and relish the source of the water in the man-made lake, I chose to stay, to stay with the continuous September rain in the ancient city X, or I chose to defer graduation or not to graduate at all, napping in classrooms now filled by truly mechanically-oriented graduate students—I had no equals because K and X were not among them—swarming from the capital to the coast, from mountains to the desert, in order to linger under and to be shielded by the archway guarded by the lush trees on campus, to study methodically intentions of the trembling trees, the very name of which I had been fooled for all these years as *French wu-tong*, until recently I found in the Chinese-English dictionary its common name *Chinese Parasol* and its scientific name *Firmiana simplex*, both of which have no entry in my *American Heritage* at all, but the latter I was finally able to locate in the *Botanica* after a fit of furious searching.

I can't help wondering if the trees were really French-grown and imported and shipped to S, and became a special class of the University of Transport. Or they were branded as French simply because to inside the barbed walls of the French settlement nearby were they decades later relocated/dislocated from its initial site in the heart of S, and spent several years there to escape the raging war fires ignited by the rising sun. The trees only to be again transported inland with the bulk of the university to X after days' overexcitements about as well as immeasurable apprehensions of their uncertain fate in the dusty wind howling through the ancient city, a cross-country relocation/dislocation by the lonesome trains set off by a monstrously poetic leap forward of the dragon in the newly crowned emperor's xenophobic dream dating back to recent colonial humiliation. The trees finally had taken root in the remains the reminder of the empire's most glorious past when X was the capital of the 1st empire, the capital of all capitals in the world, to lead an alternative life, a difficult but nevertheless life-affirming life. Or the name *French* merely signifies peacocks' nostalgia about their French horns blown by the coastal breeze, under the handsome maple-like foliage and long racemes of yellow-green flowers and curious leaf-like pods in the bund of S. Or nostalgia about Baudelaire's French whores who had traveled to S from Paris pubs. Or simply a goldfish's fantasy about French guards against the external purging waves, in their lotus dream in the lake built at the then-treeless and weed-rampant grave site in the suburb of X, where the buried poetic soul of J from the Tang Dynasty has been for more than 1,000 years assiduously planting bamboos and whispering

Do not say their roots are still weak,
Do not say their shade is still small.

All those trees and shadows of trees chase circle laugh at me wherever I go. I, the rootless floating stump of residual disorientation.

I must have been confused about season and situation. I must have confused memory with battery with scenery. I must have confused the earthly tree trunks with the magic cudgel of the Monkey King journeying to the west. I must have confused the discolored tree trunks with the blindfolded uppercase *Is*, or the headless lowercase *is*. All those trees with deceptive sexual orientations. I must have confused gender with genre. I must have confused avant-garde with Viagra. I must have confused maternity with modernity with materiality. I must have confused paper with wood with water with flesh with marble with metal.

A nanoscale doubly clamped single-crystal GaAs beam capacitively coupled to an Al single-electron transistor to test the Uncertainty Principle above the sub-atomic world.

The uncertainty of naming.

SHE: What a poe-tree! Damn incredible stamina. It must not have been embalmed for ages.

She pulls the trigger while I am still miscalculating the range of the grand cannons of poetry. Scandi – navia, you – are – the – character – in the 2nd – story, I sigh with unprecedented relief. Bullets of *yeses* shoot straight at the roof. I escaped the massacre by a nanometer. The abrasive hail of *yeses* tears up the roof decorated with oil-painted Bloody Mary. She swallows and swallows. The sonic waves of *amen*. I swallowed the purest lie and have held it intact in my stomach for so long. Don't swallow, they are infected. Yes, I blow it again. Into the cuspate valley between pages of my *American Heritage*.

There's no other place to go, no elsewhere.

Face-up she flings back onto the periodic table.

My head rolls off the periodic table, bounces up and down before finally suspended at rest in the air cleaving to the holed roof, as if suddenly filled with hydrogen or helium. It finally frees itself from the table, the periodicity, the gripping black hands, so that it can develop disembodied thinking, so that it can achieve the greatest degree of concentration. Or it frees the body's natural motion. It declares to the body, I've parted from naked you, hands, legs, and everything in-between. Part or pant, plot or polyglot, the sheer mention of it makes me fart rabidly, the trapped lead-free gas escaping through cracked teller's window's tiny single slit on the thick wall of the melting pot of memory.

SHE: I'm a black bird.

Dark matter. White page. Gray scale mask in the way of passing photoresist-curing irradiation to generate intricate patterns with feature size less than 100 nm in Si in a single step.

I am strumming *amoroso* the purple strings of her mahogany violin on note A, with my magic bow. On the giant periodic table in her conic cave on the topmost story above the Panic Station, which is cantilevered from the cliff edge overlooking the seashore, I am strumming *Camel Fantasia. I_3.* I am positive.

The painted sunflower emitting gold on the sidewall. A half-moon glass aperture agape on the roof as if the sky were still in shock. The record player spinning. Butterfly fluttering on and off the windowsills. Seabirds chirping outside the windows. She is closed, still, glued onto the periodic table. My eyes follow the rapidly changing patterns of the butterfly wings.

What's her element?

She asks again after a long interval of repose, a long pause of close listening to the birds.

I: The tanning mark left by the repeated overdoses of X-rays. The lithographic masks completely transparent to the rays of X because the usual 1,000 nm thickness of gold absorber is far too thin to effectively absorb X-rays. These misaligned gold-deficient masks have stuck on my face for too long, therefore they *are* my face, without proper repairing by pulsed caresses of the monochromic coherent visible light through stimulated emission.

She presses on.

I: From the French kiss by an apparition in the station of the metro. The stations. How was the empty space filled between all the stations?

Yes, yes, yes, I'm positive.

> *Dear S:*
>
> *But I was seized by this inexplicable disease during the intermission of the play Death of a Troubadour I was watching after sending you the badly translated Baudelaire poem during the conference break. A disease of expanding distance, of inarticulateness and*

incommunicability. A disease contracted from the gothic play, or from

our reckless free play and endless foreplay? Didn't Aristotle say that

man is an animal fond of play? I had to withdraw prematurely from

the National Council of Nanotechnology Initiatives to catch the train

home after treatment of the mysterious high fever in the emergency

room. Are you contagious? What is the name of the virus?

Yes, it was positive. I signed Yours Truest Truly and clicked brother Mouse pointing at the *cancel* button on the shining day of July. It is once again the National Day to celebrate the festival of freedom or declaration. The tragedy in my motherland—no, I can't. My dream was dashed by the gunmetal din of national anthems from the fanatic crowds and sank into the smoke from explosions outside the emptied Panic Station. I had barely escaped the infection of HIV (Humanity Intercourse Virus) at home, since the virus source, separated by the ocean, having never learnt to swim freestyle, was too distant to pose any immediate threat, only to catch its most potent form on this capital-intensively cultivated land. Damn it. One world under dog. One tongue speaks for all. I wonder if I have wasted 20 years of my lopsidedly informed precocious adulthood to finally discover the truth of the greatest promise. The butcher's truth. That must be the day I the 3rd was 1st born. The shining day in July. One month after the shining day in June, two months after the shining day in May. What are the unannounced connections beyond the expressionlessly identical numerical shade of the 2nd digits between these far-apart dates?

Was it from the fingerprinting or the X-ray detector at the customs inspection station? Not likely. Since the visa seal stamped on my freshly annealed buttock says two months after July. Or I may have gotten it from the blood test when I went to the student health service for a physical examination to fulfill registration requirements for aliens. But that's even later, deep into September.

Or P? Shane? But to this day I've not received another message from him across the ocean, neither from her who was said to have settled down in the south sometime after our last meeting, let alone any unmediated bodily contact.

There's no Amitabha in the south.

SHE: You never know.

I may well have wrongly blamed Sophia, considering all her innocence, which insisted retreating to the damp feminine (not yet certified by NIST) concavity of anion secured in the lattice point in the Ion House, even when the moon still hung quarter-way across the sky. But I have always been helplessly drawn to freshmen and sophomores. Freshmania speeches and sophomoric phrases not yet molded by the moldy curriculums.

18 = shape; 17 = taste; 16 = touch; 15 = sound;
14 = earth; 13 = water; 12 = fire; 11 = air.

Never fallen for juniors or seniors and any ladders above. Even the idea of the number 20 or numbers 20ish appalls me. Does that mean I will forever be a freshman, or worse, a sophomore, in any field or career, be it chosen self-consciously, which is rare, or more often trapped in it by circumstances?

Even though I have shamelessly bagged in my knapsack 8 diplomas and certificates in 4 disciplines and 4 languages from 6 institutions among 500 universities I have attended, consecutively, or simultaneously, however brief in duration.

I say, I merely mastered the method. The method of counting, coping, counterfeiting, and castrating. Teeth of helical, conical involute, spiral bevel, and hypoid gears, and cylindrical rollers of heavy-duty roller bearings in the received ideological machines in the recycled moral system. The method of statistical sampling and confidence estimation. Found numbers of unnatural deaths, and jammed numbers of foreign shortwave radio frequencies. In the last analysis it is method that counts. Everything else cunts. Everything cunts.

To go back to your earlier question about my age, I am 9, 1, and 1, an odd sequence of numerical events, odd numbers, positive numbers, rational numbers. I was never given a chance to mature. But if you carry out elementary arithmetic operations on every possible combination of these numbers, it might as well be even, prime, fractional, zero, negative, or irrational. I am not just a baby even in a purely numerical sense. All answers are true depending on which I you are really into, and your point of view, that is your method of calculation.

With each newborn I, I grew further inwards from a hollow sphere like consecutive shrinking concentric spherical shells approaching a vanishing dot in the center, which will be I the 4th, or I the ultimate, I in the last version, which sounds, looks, feels very much like the pure Iron. Silvery white, lustrous, malleable, ductile, conducting, and magnetic up to a curious temperature. My existence beyond numbers. Take my words, this is not a metaphor.

But my outer, my previous selves, never relent their grips on my newer inner self, and they, while being continually oxidized, corroded, pounded, only harden and thicken and press more after each new birth.

Me, or my head, that is my body, a steel ball of abstraction with tender thin layers within thick hard layers within even thicker and harder layers, with increasing carbon concentration along the outward normal direction, as a result of the decelerated inward carbon diffusion of soot of burnt but never completely buried dreams of dreams and cinders of burning memories of dreams of dreams.

> *Dear S:*
>
> *Are you the 48 slip systems in α iron or the never-melt hexagonal close-*
>
> *packed plate-like or column-like snowflakes on the mountaintop?*

Or symbolically $I = \sum_i w_i I_i$, where w_i is the time-dependent weight whose functional form is contingent on the particular mechanisms operating in the birth process, with $\sum_i w_i = 1$, i being positive integers from 1 to 3. I am talking about the mass. All the *I*s no matter how far the index i runs amount only to *is*.

SHE: What is *is*?

Not Si.
Not Si.
Is is not Si.

Is it the *is* that follows it in an affirmative sentence or the *is* that precedes it in a general interrogative? Or is the *is* merely a misspelling of *it*? So is it.

Say it. Say *it*.

SHE: What is it?

It is not Ti (Titanium), is it?

It is nor TI (Texas Instruments), is it?

It is?

It is hot.

It is raining.

How many *Is* are necessary for the existence of *us*? What are the latent heat of fusion and the melting point for the crystalline *Is* to become the liquid *we*? *When we meet again*, isn't it the way we used to sing?

Without exception I became addicted to them all. To all these ws and Is. Helplessly. With the deliberate exception of I_0 and w_0, my primitive form and weight, for the time being, since the birth of I_0 was too remote and the particulars of the circumstances are still too opaque to me to have immediate impact upon my present story.

SHE: Another intriguing story.

Here's a synopsis. The amniotic fluid of my philosophy major ma conceived me in a swirl of raucous parades on the boulevard of flags. On the shining day in May, four years after the General Theory of Relativity for the gravitational force was presented. In the height of the '60s when she was still at the sweet even age of 16, I was born in a clay cave, where no light bulbs were needed due to its closeness to the embankment of the draught dam, whose surface glittered with slogans of *damnation*, among dunes of negative sentences and blacklists. Oil lamps and candles, the 1st lights in my primitive life. It is in the desert where I was born, where the sun never stopped guffawing at night, where the capitalized sun never explained during the day, where particles of love had no room to dwell. I the preliminary, or I_0, the 1st-born, was born into ideas of *production* and *reproduction* of steel, from abused soil, from mucks and carcasses of domestic animals and deprived humans in the 9th category, from ashes of burned libraries, from shards of destroyed temples. I_0 must have come out of her rectum, judging by her frequent intestine spasms and the filthy taste of my earliest memory. I was a born protester. I_0 was spellbound in the ooze of *class* and *classification* in the dam bed with my only pink friend *investigation* searching for the impossible blackbird of *liberation* in the sky of *incantation* of steel maxims. Abstruse words always made me jump and roll like a loose ball. While waiting for the ritual of initiation I_0 danced and danced with no feeling for half a decade in the barracked but shaky middle school classrooms, with the pulp images of the *Gang of Four*, that is *south, east, north*, and *west*, big impersonal characters lifted from yellowed newspapers and torn posters whining cynically behind the suddenly eclipsed sun danced until my torso twisting without tearing apart into a lotus shape sank into the slush.

SHE: 60 carbon atoms in Buckminsterfullerene C_{60} printed out of the Epson Stylus C60 inkjet printer?

60 ways of pointing fingers at the sun. In the tiny triangle formed by both hands, I_0 handed ma the 1st 60 pennies earned by planting 60 six-foot-tall aspen trees on the barren loessial mound in a day, in his childish whim to count to 60, to weigh 60, to find 60 secret links between copper and wood, to adjure 60 times rain forest to the desert, even though he was too wretched with his thorny head to be received by any circle of villagers, too little to go to school, too little to imagine the full range and depth of the devastation's penetration, in the wake of the unprecedented storm sweeping the nation, which was yet to recover from the previous catastrophe of tens of millions of unnatural human losses only six years earlier—6, a truly menacing number, and therefore 3, since $6 = 3 + 3$, since 3 is the number of years of the worst losses sustained in the catastrophe—as a result of the emperor's yet another chimera to multiply and consolidate his personal empire.

And my father's repeatedly recounting his cubic disgust *what an unsightly head* at his 1st sight of the firstborn's cuboid head six months after birth in the cubic clay cave.

Because it is impossible for a cube of a whole number to be written as the sum of two cubes of whole numbers.

I say, So my 1st name *Abstract*, so my initial *A*, so my anonym *A*. And my obsession with my ma. My one and only singular ma. Don't ever 2nd-guess my ma. Yes, I am positive. I was destined to be born for the 3rd time from the shining July day on, long after the solid state death of me the 2nd, as the poet with metal's melancholy.

Via an **M** transformation, I say. No, it got to be a **P**-type.

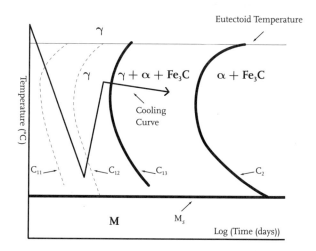

Figure 1: A Poet's Representation of TTT Diagram for the Emotional Microstructures of Low Carbon Steel.

Eutectoid transformation: Temperature at which two solid phases form from one.

γ *(austenite = autism)*: solid solution of C (carbon) in fcc (face-centered cubic) iron.

α *(ferrite = fury)*: solid solution of C in bcc (body-centered cubic) iron.

Fe$_3$C *(cementite = sentiment)*: iron carbide with 6.67% C.

P *(pearlite = parataxis)*: lamellae of α and **Fe$_3$C**.

M *(martensite = matricide)*: a bct (body-centered tetragonal) supersaturated α with excessive carbon.

M_s: start temperature for γ–**M** transformation.

C curves: a family of curves that mark the start (C_1: C_{11}, C_{12}, C_{13}), finish (C_2), and intermediate points of transformation at a given temperature. Also called TTT (time-temperature-transformation) diagram.

C_{11}: east coast of the ancient land.

C_{12}: west coast of the promised land. (Cause for 1st right shift: precious metals rising from sunken ships of dead dynasties on the ocean floor)

C_{13}: east coast of the promised land. (Cause for 2nd right shift: floods of right-alloying elements in the air of promise)

C_2: polynomial interpolation of coastlines of Norway, France, Portugal, Western Sahara, and South Africa.

I_2–γ Transformation:

Mechanism: Rapid diffusion via 10-hours heating above-eutectoid temperature by supersonic friction between the airplane body skin and the atmospheric turbulence, heightened expectation and sensation.

Percentage of Transformation Completed: 100%.

γ–P Transformation:

Mechanism: Slow diffusion due to rapid cooling below and subsequent heating back up to the γ–P region. It includes nucleation and growth. The incubation period of nucleation can be calculated by Scheil's method, the phase growth an Avrani type equation, based on C_1 and C_2.

(Reasons for γ–M suppression: The above-eutectoid γ plummeted to below eutectoid temperature during my 1st landing in the new world, with the fast cooling curve completely missing C_1, more due to C_1's faster rightward shifting; yet the temperature was higher than M_s, because I fell out of the airplane to my knee onto an abstruse plane, mathematically flat, groundless, ground-proof, to be grounded, not to be ground, yet never to have been truly grounded, so the landing ground was no ground at all, in the sense that the ground is a foundation for something else, nor aboveground because everything else is above me, let alone underground because I could never understand, nevertheless, a kind of middle ground between the earthly ground and poetic ground, a battleground—yet I again aligned with the orderly traffic flow of rainbows of flags, yon I audited rhythms of gyrating hips and bellies, yes I was astonished at the aroma of plots of lush verdure among high-raising structures, yet I again anointed the earth if only its discrete surface asperities, yes I assayed the strange sweetness of the ellipsoid ball, yes I was arrested by conceptual flowers of many degrees of freedom unaware of the background weeds of PowerPoint— foregrounding γ's grinding forever the abrasive dense surface air flow of capitals and therefore generating abstract frictional heat, thus combined with drastically reduced convection achieving a new equilibrium temperature, higher than M_s, staying cool and cooling *largo*.

Circumstances for potential γ–**M** however do exist: a blizzard; a deep recession; the rise of any extremisms; the spreading of New Formalism.

Do look out for signs of embedded tempered **M**.)

Percentage of Transformation Completed: slight. **P** has barely began to form after nanoparticles of I_3's feeble voice had been kept from bursting out in the matrix of metastable autistic γ in a decade of incubation, in which there existed no any indexed *I*s at all, or I simply I, or the super cool super-cooled homogeneous γ, and at the end of which ma finally muscled to release the fetus of careerless retarded I_3, in her longest if not the last fart across the ocean, across the ocean of time, her cunt too worn out to open again, to help abate her decade-old fresh pain in the ass.

SHE: What stories and days of incubation?

Every day I strive to detect microstructures of this phallic column of Time with laser ultrasonics—days of mooing cows, blunt *how*s, and mad *now*s, days of my random walks in the Ion House, days of daily periodic rate of 0.05477% (or 19.99% APR); every night sleepless I count with all my fingers and toes untold stories in the multi-colored head of the Empire Building; day and night by brutal force approach with primitive faith I crunch random numbers for the spatial coordinates of the Time Square on the supreme IBM computer.

But for a while, I_3 slept, swallowed prayers, and shitted lists as if performing daily secular rituals on the concrete *New York stool* with roundness-craving *vowel*s and digressing *yowl*s to implore the receding flesh of the *fat whole, flat hole,* and *curved canon.*

Will my golden moment ever be back again?

SHE: In the village or the Valley National Bank?

I say, On the periodic table of the elements in the Ion House. Work nano, think ionic. That is to map the whereabouts of Shane, who stylized himself with the same hairdo as Sophia but who was far more eloquent in Chinese, which Sophia could hardly speak at all, and whom I met by chance at the Korean section of a periodically modulated ethnic dinner table in the Ion House, where I occupied a single room on the top story with a magnificent view of the SiO_2 Bridge before my eventual sliding down the Silicon Valley.

I had been for months deeply unsettled by the phrase *sort of seeing*, or could it be *short of seeing*, in Sophia's answer to my persistent inquisition into her relationship with another anion. Sophia, a political science sophomore from Lost Angel, or Lost Soul, with the missing vowel *e*, whose voice resembled remarkably the tight-lipped statue in the Square in our conversation about Dostoyevsky's brothers during the orientation tour across the bay across the bridge for new residents, half of whom were host anions like herself and the other half interstitial foreign cations like me, in a nearly but never perfect charge equilibrium throughout the Ion House, which is always slightly positive because cations have lost more electrons than anions can accommodate in their closely packed cubic unit cells so that they never form a truly stable crystal structure, i.e., short of long-range order, yet with sort of short-range order, therefore might as well be characterized as a quasi-crystal when examined from a short distance with the tainted scope of *sort of seeing, sort of*, the subtle meanings of which had been proffered to me by P, and again by Shane later.

P, over whom I prevailed in the final of the intramural table tennis tournament, who immediately became my training partner afterwards, whose technique was a letterpress reprint of that of a younger and not-yet-matured-technically X at the table, but physically who resembles the lanky K, and more so in terms of their passions in classical music and vernaculars, in spite of their differences in color. This likeness between P and K always appears to me as images of the continuous PK (Penalty Kick) battle, with P and K alternating the role as kicker and goalkeeper, to determine who the winner is after a tied regular period of the World Cup soccer games, which we used to watch well into dawn in the ancient city. But P's insights into mechanisms of friction between polymer surfaces revolutionized my grasp of spin in Ping-Pong and raised my game to another level overnight. The magic spin.

Sort of, or *somewhat, a little, moderately, considerably,* the exact extent to which she was involved with the other refused to reveal itself to me, since I did not yet own a copy of the most authoritative edition of the *American Heritage,* or it simply had not yet been in circulation then, and the meanings still elude me today even though I have the 4th edition with me wherever I go, and therefore none of them has ever led me beyond my initial confusion, their contradictory explanations, explanations which now I suspect have been deliberately orchestrated.

Because $\overset{15}{\underset{\substack{Phosphorus \\ 30.973761(2)}}{P}}$ and $\overset{16}{\underset{\substack{Sulfur \\ 32.065(5)}}{S}}$ are next-door neighbors on the same story in the periodic table, differing by only one electron, while $\overset{53}{\underset{\substack{Iodine \\ 126.90447(3)}}{I}}$ has more electrons (53) than P and S combined (15 + 16), since S is a native of volcanoes and hot springs of emotion along the Gulf Coast, pale yellow, odorless, crucial in synthesis of fertilizers and black gunpowder and rubber vulcanization, and P an essential component of living systems and found in nervous tissue, bones, and cell protoplasm, extracted from urine, existing in several allotropic forms, white (or yellow), red, and black (or violet), the white one catching fire spontaneously in air, a fact that enables P and S to produce exciting variations in play, forming numerous phosphorus sulfides, while I, bluish-black, with radioactive isotopes like I-129 abundant in nuclear waste with a half-life of more than 10 million years, with an irritating odor, offers no appealing attributes at all, though I works quietly in internal biochemical processes as a mode of protection against invasion by foreign chemicals and organisms. Yet the associations between P, S, and I are neither entirely poetically unpredictable, because we are all entangled and contained, even with different period and/or group numbers, in the same probe wave packet (i.e., block).

So that after two months with Sophia in daily email chats, at dinners on Telenet Ave, and Kurosawa films at the Art Museum, unable to sort out the intention of *sort of*, I was again eating alone on the Korean table in the Ion House, when Shane turned to me and seemingly walked in my direction, blowing on his way the fervent English horn with black Irish coffee, kissing the wailing guitar of the drunken king of Spain, and I was less and less assured about the true position of his intention as he walked faster and faster to my table of kimchi of xylophone in the far corner, rubbing elbows with spaghetti-stuffed yodeling beasts from Italy, paying no respect to the Norwegian queen and songs of wild strawberries, unhearing the Ghanian chant of grilled chicken, uttered in fluent Mandarin *is this a Chinese chair?* hard, hoarse, but carrying extra heat that was cold, like the sound of *Martensite* relieving its strain of innermost fear at room temperature—every fear begins at room temperature—in the arabesquely staged dining hall by cracking out loud, and sat next to me, like a Martian, like the big and squat and reddish cowboy in the old western, horseless and bootless, instantly commandeering the entire restive stable.

Strange I've met neither K nor X in the Ion House. Not strange because K or Potassium is located so far apart at the other end of the periodic table across the vast valley of transition metals while X does not appear at all, because X was never fond of Chemistry and its pungent empirical smell.

SHE: More oil, how does friction choke the course of fiction?

I: Less love.

Once I accidentally found a book from the dust-covered shelf, which permanently perturbed the *three points* and *one line* of my life. Every time I tried to dig up water from the oil well in our safari into the desert, an unnamable inflammation spoiled all my efforts; without a word she shut up and closed the leather-jacketed book, turned around and away from me and entered the fog, leaving me alone with fresh burns. I ripped off the cover entitled *The Book of Forespoken Machines*, or *The Book of Foreshortened Infinite Series*, or *The Book of Foreskinned Lights*, or *The Book of Forbidden Foreign Names*, or *The Book of Forgotten Letters*, or *The Book of Forsaken Songs*, the cover with pictures of headless figures crossing a nameless road, abstractly engraved caves, or suns, multiple suns in different diameters and illuminations set afire on top of a green-eyed whore on the undulant surface of the sea, only to be baffled every time by its original title page *The Theory of Spin*, and I lay face-down on the disarrayed table of contents on the trembling writing table, tearing page after page from the book, forming and reforming impossible lines, dressing the chipped TiC-coated drill-bit with my desk-top synthesized diamond grinding wheel, dressing my new ferrous wound. 1st in the Science Library in the ancient city. 2nd in the History Library in the capital. 3rd in the Library of Witchcraft within walking distance from the Ion House.

Dear S:

Are you the surface-alloyed martyr or the salad of roasted French tree

barks topped with freedom dressing?

SHE: What was it?

Wounds never commute with their afflicters. Or words. Or so I always believe. *You hurt my feelings*, P whispered into my right ear Shane's grievance in the smoky Bare Bar, at rest out of phase with me by 180° after spinning around and around on the high chair. About my not returning his repeated calls right before he went back again to the capital within months of the defense of his dissertation on *Antimatters*, not to teach again PSL (Physics as a Spiritual Language) in the Academy, but to study PSL (Physique as a Sign Language) at the College of Fashion, and to play again alto sax in the trendy bars, more likely I figure to resume his ex-exploration during his 1st stint in the capital, which was cut short abruptly by the catastrophe.

The image of the paper phallus swaying on my outside door handle the morning after our night-long conversation in my cubic room in the Ion House has been troubling me to no end.

I say, By the rapid fire-exchange of *touch probe, 1st down, finite deformation, sidespin*, in English, Chinese, and Greek way, between Shane and me, after a vegetarian dinner in his entropic apartment filled by popular songs from the '80s, after the premier in the Art Museum of the new documentary about the catastrophe.

Uninhibited exchanges, as continuation of our table talk, about terracotta warriors escaping the mausoleum of the 1st emperor, the silver cross hanging on the rose-apple tree under which Buddha 1st came into being, qi and alternate current, advances and retreats across the stretched line of scrimmage, across the triangular and quadrilateral 2nd-order interpolated ABAQUS mesh of midnight, across the silk net of Ping-Pong game of *Forrest Gump*, the fishnet with such large pores that through which sleek word fish slipped at will never caught, accusations like *did you regret not having done it with him in the Ion House* or *was it a women you were in love with in the capital*, proposals like *give me the gun*, which I refused, because of our opposite charges, yes I regretted immediately, yes I was too frightened by the possibility of unexpected ring, like the ultimatum from loudspeakers in the wee hours of the morning, and thus immediate realization of the possibility through my unfounded fear when the phone rang, when Sophia invited me to watch *Diamond and Ashes* in her room, which I turned down, citing my coming exam as a sort of sorry excuse, words of *sort of*, words of the life here, of the life there, of the lives of our beasts, of the atrocious lives of our ages, of local forms of catastrophe, of our definitive body trajectories through the catastrophe, which strangely didn't physically intersect at all even we happened to be physically in the same Academy at the time, albeit unknowing each other, nevertheless understandable considering the different languages we spoke then, the immense heat damage zone in the capital, and the unprecedented students' t-distribution of the multi-dimensional random variables of the catastrophe, or the unreliability of memories of my senses for being either too old since I_1 was still on its way to sudden death in the catastrophe or too young because I_2 was yet to be out of ma's sick body until after the catastrophe.

The catastrophe of the overly simplified theory.

SHE: What is it?

To reformulate my number theory of the catastrophe of the theory of finding chronological roots of '80s blunders, barring typographical errors, round-off errors, random errors, and truncation errors, I_1 lingered before ma ma's square youth in the height of '60s projected in the 8×10 photo portrait since the product gives 80. '60s way, threaded by the even number 60, the including angle of the equilateral triangle on a Euclidean plane, the passing grade for the deadly real-time course *Political Education.*

$60 = 30 \times 2 =$ days of open mourning and protest before curfew $\times$ demands in the hunger strike manifesto $= 20 \times 3 =$ date of martial law's enforcement $\times$ sides of triangle $= 15 \times 4 =$ days from declaration of martial law to the massacre $\times$ sides of square $= 12 \times 5 =$ prime hours of violence $\times$ the senses $= 10 \times 6 =$ level of pain based on a scale of 1 to 10$\times$ square faces of the imperial cube $= 5 \times 4 \times 3 =$ senses $\times$ square $\times$ triangle $= 5 \times 3 \times 2 \times 2 =$ senses $\times$ triangle $\times$ endpoints of a hard line segment $\times$ parties needed for a constructive dialogue

Oh multiplication, what a monstrous operation.

Yet we have $60 = 7 + 53 = 13 + 47 = 17 + 43 = 19 + 41 = 23 + 37 = 29 + 31$, six ways of writing 60 in sum of two primes. Seven demands were listed in their initial petition; the hunger strike began on the 13th day of the month; she was 17 when I_1 saw her stand there; 19th was the date when the invasion was launched; it was reported on the 23rd of March that 250,000 marched in the city against the invasion. It's no coincidence that both 2003 and 89 are prime numbers. Or crime numbers. What do the rest of these primes imply?

What are the sinister connections between addition and multiplication?

SHE: What is it?

The birth of tragedy = triangle.

Defaulting his teaching duties in the Academy, Shane frequented the poster-flooded triangle area in the Conservatory, and the English triangle in the nearby park, to check the parity of the party of P and the like, instead he found mandarin-speaking Paganinis giving him free lessons on triangular fire in a peaceful revolution.

While the equilateral triangle KXI emerged 1st in my mind's drafting paper a year after they left X, from the triangle formed by X, S, and the capital, when I drew straight lines between them on the country map, during the research field trip from X to S then to the capital and back to X, to refine the scope of my thesis *Micromechanics of Fatigue of Low Carbon Martensite Steel.*

Then again on the train home in mid-June after we saw X off at the airport to Stockholm a year after that, when I was visually measuring through the Euclidian window in the passenger's cabinet space between fleeting aspen trees alongside the railway, upright aspen trees which straightened the warped vacant space around me, and listening to the soliloquy of the trees in the wind, which soothed spasmodic grunts of fatigued engine, worn wheels, and the unknown force bursting my chest.

Ever since back to the capital, she had been hooked to performances at the capital's esteemed Conservatory, of *39th, 40th, 41st, Four Seasons,* off from work at NIST (National Institute of Standards and Technology), the nation's establisher, arbitrator, and administrator of all technical standards, but by default indifferent to any humanity standards, where she was pursuing interferometric measurement of *Cylindricity*—a surface of revolution in which all points of the surface are equidistant from a common axis, inspired by the idea of observing proton decay in a cylindrical tank buried 1,000 meters underground in Kamioka, Japan, filled with 50,000 tons of water. Since our 1st meeting at the concrete table in X he had never been able to drive Ping-Pong out of his schedule, though he was tied by machine tool designs to the drafting board since his relocation from S to the capital soon after my arrival. Since leaving X for the capital with my fatigued *Martensite* three years after our parting in X, I had become the latest defector from *Micromechanics* to the experimental project *Mirco-melancholy* at the Academy of Since, the new independent think tank.

A capitalized triangle formed by three straight lead lines. Lines we had drawn on the apparent surface of the capital during our day-long 1st reunion from far-apart corners in the suburb. 1st the initial thin lines tentatively with the H pencil that is hard and resists wear and therefore you must press hard, 2nd the intermediate lines with the HB pencil that is mild and serves general writing purpose, assuring they are aligned with the initial lines, and 3rd the terminal lines over the intermediate lines, applying gentle pressure with the B pencil since it is soft and wears off readily, to give them a more solid finishing touch with a line width of 3 mm. Lead lines as a way of holding the world in our hands, as a way of leading us through the four loops surrounding the capital. Lead lines that we were soon to leave completely to floods of the moment, not knowing what we'd missed when they disappeared, only to awake to the seriousness of the loss in our 2nd reunion at the desolate moat bank a month after that, vowing to draw and redraw the triangle and never again leave it undermaintained.

SHE: Where is it?

It has protracted and softened. From the equilateral triangle with cm-size sides on the drafting plane with 180° sum of including angles to the spherically curved obtuse triangles with 10,000-mile-long sides stretching across oceans with larger-than-180° sum of including angles. No. It has shrunk and stiffened. From the almost equilateral triangle of 10-mile-long sides in the capital to blank scalene triangles of mm-size between lines of my unwritten disjointed stories. Yes. It has time-traveled from the elliptic space in the last century of the past millennium to the hyperbolic space in the new one, in which the sum of including angles of a triangle is always less than 180°. It must. To offset the angular defects.

11 of them. To make the sum total to the expectation value 1980.

But similar triangles do not exist in hyperbolic space.

Who would bother poetry if love reciprocated every time in real time?

SHE: Keep going, A.

Fleeing the chaotic scenes in the back room of the Bare Bar, I_3 stumbled into the twilight and smoked some black pot from a redheaded hum in the People's Park, 60 miles north from the industrial park. What immediately followed escapes my memory. Oops, a short-circuit in my flushed neural network.

SHE: Lighter, slow down, A-. You are hurting me, my eardrums. Move up a bit, more circular motion.

I lower the pitch and tempo of the music from note F to A from *allegro* to *andante*, to feel the contours of my feeling. Dear ma, what's the shape of the wound I afflicted on you in your delivering the concrete me the 2nd in the emergency room? Elliptic or trapezoidal or rectangular? Or was it too triangular?

But every time I ran an experiment to reproduce the nanoscale perfect triangle in Si with advanced X-ray lithography in the clean room, all I got was, instead of the solid equilateral triangle with vertices K, X, and I, an isosceles triangle with absurdly long equal sides of dotted lines, vertices severely blurred. Is something intrinsically wrong in the controlled experimental conditions or basic assumptions of the experiments? Or is nanoscience just another nonsensical scientific venture?

Peculiar isosceles triangles, my wounds. Lithographic witness of the pretentiousness of similes. Atomic testimony to the impossibility of metaphors.

> *Dear S:*
>
> *Are you atomically smooth?*

I have been secretly investigating the technical viability of and devising methodologies for, in the true literal sense of poetics, *direct writing*, which is maskless, therefore mask-related-error-free, sequential thus slow in throughput, and targeting only application-specific readers, who are numbered and whose reading patterns behave too erratically to justify the expense of mask production. I revised and revised my proposal and submitted and resubmitted it to NSF (National Science Foundation) and was rejected every time. One reason is dubious intention. Another reason is point contacts with technological and economic reality. Yet another unjustified spending budget with lack of adequate institutional support and a critical mass. Yet another too negligible a likelihood of success to merit support.

SHE: That's right.

I left home, whatever that means, the clean room too, after all those drafting years
of three points and one line, three points of because and therefore and one line of
anyway, and embarked on my hypothetical journey in search of the royal concrete,
the concrete vertices of the abstract triangle, accompanied by my American Heritage.
I took trains, or hitchhiked, whichever was convenient. I'd been forced to surrender
my driver's license long ago, after time and again straying lane by lane from the
right lane to the left on my way across the divider, and into the left lane on the
other side of the road where there always seemed to be much less traffic, except
when I was trapped in a single lane downtown with neither left to turn towards nor
right to turn away from, not to move forward faster, not because I couldn't stand
or didn't want to understand my right of way, not because I tried to escape the grip
of the troubleshooter of all the wrong turns in gear trains, not because I had given
up any hope of arriving at the right place at the right time, not that I was led by
the left-hand circularly polarized headlight, that I was born without a right brain,
that I'm a lefty with a natural advantage in Ping-Pong, that I was a victim of the
periodic floods on the left bank of the river of polluted dogmas and corrupted data
files, that I left and left and left, that I felt and felt and felt the felt mat under my
unfeeling feet, but overwhelmed by the illusion that I was driving backwards in time
writing road sentences in reverse to tame the monster of the infinitely regressive
machine, to move towards unknown forefathers, the living dead pacing to and fro
on the swept boulevard, that I was driving on the left bank of the Seine River arguing
aloud with French deconstructionists to pin down the last French Wutong tree as if
it had ever existed at all, after having been constantly frustrated by the congested
flow of motorized people heading headlong from womb to tomb, by the endless
roadwork signs along my computer-generated route, as if the road were only the
site of eternal roadwork instead of the way of passage, like the repeatedly breached

road maps towards impossible peace. Though only after I had swallowed without any digestion the multitudes of limbless motionless *I*s suspended in mid air on I-1, I-5, I-15, I-80, I-95, I-85, I-75, I-10, again and again crisscrossing this forever-foreign land, since I did all my driving in the sweet dreams of the deepest nights when I could see nothing of the cities and towns except the vague triangular outlines of unnamable treetops and regularly spaced cubes of identical indifferent gas stations under different names, when trucks with heavy pain load unanimously gave way to my wildly nimble Accord Coupe, when officers were off-duty. I became a screwed driver, screwed by the cold rolling of highway patrol officers after sunrise, by thread cutting of uninsured drunken drivers under moonlight, by shot peening of snipers lurking in the rain. The rain never stopped from Athens to Atlanta to Avenue A. The solar wind turns its head into a tail out of fear or shame or gross confusion above the sky of Santa Monica, Yuma, Tularosa, Victoria, Alexandria, Columbia, Tuscaloosa, and Tampa. Where are you reading tonight? I became a screwdriver, driving clockwise downwards round-headed, flat-headed, oval-headed, and Fillister-headed right-handed stiff analytical screws revolutionary screws into every visible pothole along my way while imagining the axis about which *Firmiana simplex* trees rotate and then parallel to which they translate to complete a perfect screw motion which will bring them to the ancient city from any corner on earth, and turning the pitted earth, fixed in the right-handed coordinate frames, into a thread-jointed and fastened whole to set my story on a solid ground, blind to its many-colored flowers, deaf to the muffled voices *screw mother earth screw mother earth* from mad dogs and the fat rat with defective heart implant furiously digging up the ground under the bushes. The CDMS II (Cryogenic Dark Matter Search) experiment employs a detector located half a mile below ground in the historic Soudan Iron Mine in northeastern Minnesota to seek signals of WIMPs (Weakly Interacting Massive Particles). Weakly interconnected to the steering wheel, I became a perpetual rider of and a master of how to ride BART, Amtrak, subway trains, and trends of the moment, and a station dweller between rides, with no hope of ever driving back again. Except in my story.

I had forgotten all about S after sending my hurried electronic note from the Panic Station, even though I carried Sophia's home address in my wallet. But I was fatally attached to a noun to which I have no clue other than the strange sounding yet remotely familiar syllable *ma*, when I roomed with monks in the largest temple in Lost Angel. Or *am* could it be. Am I I am? I am am I? *Am* or *ma*. One way or the other or both ways.

Exotic nouns, my constant enemy and my obsession.

SHE: A non?

No, a noun in the chant. Not a noun without you.

SHE: A nan?

Out of the question. There's no Amitabha in the south. South, nonstop news briefings of saturation bombing.

SHE: A nun, oh Lord?

But a nun is nothing but a noun with the elliptic story of oxygen.

SHE: A, did . . . ?

In my daydreams.

Dear S:

Are you the strayed subject desperately looking for the lost object

or otherwise?

Camping alone deep in the heart of the Death Valley off the wireless off-ramp of the interstate information superhighway to recover my sobriety, I conversed with masters of words. One claimed, Stories are the only things we have in life. A story is nothing but the set of *rooms* on the same level of a building. Under the dim moonlight I traced my *American Heritage* again.

The tiny digits of my footprints of self-exiled
what why of a shifty *he she it*, with ill-timed
had been would have been could have been should have been
and sacred, reluctant, sacred, reluctant
fall prostrate flow struggle stumble squeal bleed stand wonder
turn forget pause stoop ponder
return remember stall supine spring,
with extravagant
theoretical transient translational,
with unhinged

along alongside after(glow)

amid among after(shock)

abreast of ahead of after(current)

apropos of as of as for as to after(blow)

aboard above atop across after(math)

at against after(trembling)

absent aside from after(image)

apart from away from after(sound)

about after(birth)

around after(burst)

along with after(heat)

as far as after(thought)

as well as after(taste)

as after(growth)

as though after(life)

as if after(world)

according to after(effect)

according as after(fact)

at the mercy of after(cause)

as long as after(time)

as a result of after(word)

although after(language)

and also after(after(after . . .))

all but after

always already after

as many times as after

{*axisymmetric, animistic, apractic, anisometric, anticlerical, axonometric, axiological, analectic, agnostic, androcentric, archaeoastronomical, astigmatic, atheistic, autocratic, astraphobic, aesthetic, abulic, anthropogenic, apotropaic, archangelic, astrological, anesthetic, anamnestic, aposiopetic, anomic, algolagnic, autobiographic, astatic, akinetic, antilogarithmic achromatic, anthropocentric, apoplectic, antonymic, alphanumerical, autodidactic, autohypnotic, architectonic, Anglophilic, Anglocentric, apneic, aperiodic, anorectic, allophonic, anharmonic, archaeological, astrodynamic, aerobic, agoraphobic, aposematic, aerodynamic, allomorphic, antipsychotic, adynamic, antipyretic, aphrodisiac, aphonic, atavistic, abapical, autogenic, anosmic, aerostatic, acerbic, atypical, animatistic, acoustic, achromic, agamic, alogical, antipathetic, apothegmatic, anaphrodisiac, Anglophobic, anagramatical, authentic, aphoristic, arrhythmic, anthological, anticlimactic, aleatoric, allegorical, anachronic, anabatic, antispasmodic, azonic, analogical, antimagnetic, aphaeretic, aoristic, artistic, anaclitic, audiological, atrophic, atresic, autoerotic, antagonistic, anthropomorphic, anaphoric, alcoholic, anarchic, arachnophobic, atheoretical, autonomic, angelic, apathetic, antiperiodic, anechoic, allographic, anthropic, ahistorical, aristocratic, asthenopic, athletic, aphotic, agonistic, archaic, agonic, Anglophonic, acrostic, acrophobic, aspheric, autographic, alchemic, algorithmic, apocalyptic, apolitical, albinistic, antithetical, aphetic, altruistic, allergic, abiological, antic, apostrophic, astrophysical, analphabetic, antinomic, apodictic, antitypical, asyntactic, acronymic, anachronistic, analgetic, anarthric, atonic, antiseptic, anagogic, ataractic, asyndetic, abiotic, adiabatic, archetypic, arctic, acrobatic, agraphic, ascetic*}* after*

after all

on the hiking trails of the expansive valley between rocky mountains of *dimension tolerance sanctum safe-sex public hearing pubic earring republic of hyperbole zill-of-rights*, my American heritage.

My American heritage never lasting more than a nanosecond, obliterated by orchestrated trampling within and without *proof fiction refinery slaughterhouse masked bedroom*, of firmly positioned black-and-white

in case of if in fear of if in danger of if

in place of if instead of if in spite of if in addition to if

in defiance of if

in preparation of if in the hope of if in want of if

in view of if in light of if in respect to if in regard to if

in relation to if in accordance with if in association with if

in conjunction with if

in favor of if in the service of if in the interests of if

in compliance with if in conformity with if

in agreement with if

in the manner of if in behalf of if in terms of if

in the name of if

in the midst of if in company of if in harmony with if

in tune with if

in connection with if in step with if in keeping with if

in line with if

in search of if in pursuit of if in quest of if in charge of if

insofar as if insomuch as if

in order that if

if only

if and only if,

of Attic *good evil*, of unchallenged *pre post*, of ever-present *am am am*, by accented obese *Is*, drumming *we*, and grunting condescended crowded *they*, and by *however whichever wherever whoever whenever*, conceited, decent-mannered, wholehearted, icy, ill-minded, or mean-spirited in unpredictable turns, or by gusts of desert storms which every time escape weathermen's bold numbers and colored charts, and my gut feelings.

The wind was strong in the capital. The wind was blowing all the words. The west wind of fingering ideas threw her out of the ambulance in the early night. The east wind of tethered objects tripped him on bicycle rushing to the scene just before dawn. While throughout the day and night I was pushed towards the foot of the campanile by the converging circular waves of mercury law, tending my devastated *ma*.

Catastrophe replicates and amplifies itself asexually and self-adaptively in different time zones. The collateral damage of catastrophe knows no boundary in time. A fault tolerant domain.

It must not be just coincidence that without exception all my failed stories ended up in a disorderly room of sorts, that my writing experiments went awry every time in the clean room. The possible sources of errors in pattern transfer with X-ray lithography: (a) X-ray source; (b) mask; (c) photoresist; (d) alignment of mask to substrate. The mechanisms of error interaction and propagation unknown.

I slow down my left arm to *adagio* and flip through the dictionary with my right foot. For the 3rd time I sum and sum up all the diagonal elements of my *American Heritage*. A room: an area separated by walls or partitions from other similar parts of the building in which it is located.

The stories on the tangent plane I have been composing, my American heritage.

I say, The room. The look on the two dozen stiff faces of the grand jury in the courtroom of the Supreme Court of Grammar two blocks from City Hall made me sick every morning until this day. Those cocksuckers in the city hall. The consultation room in the mental institution a month after the catastrophe, where the doctor repeatedly barked *which of you needs help* the moment K, X, and I rolled in arranged neatly in a row. No spirits of dogs survived the terrifying regularity of campaigns to weed out *spiritual contamination,* and the freshly whetted stainless steel knives on the hot pottery plates.

Into the deepest water of the lake Prof. Z waded, under his belt thick textbooks and lecture notes and ungraded student homework full of unanswered unanswerable abstract algebra questions, muttering *at least, at the least, at the very least, Least Squares,* and disappeared without a trace, after an extended conversation with me during his office hours in the main building for instruction, following the onset of the short-lived 3rd campaign by the new emperor.

Only less than four years after the discovery of Z boson at CERN, which, with a mean life of 3×10^{25} second, heavier than an iron atom, electrically neutral, is its own antiparticles, and is the carrier particle that mediates the weak force that does not involve charge and flavor changes via a neutral current, leaving interacting particles unaffected, except a transfer of momentum.

Concrete, I howled to the desert wind. Dust rained down far faster, denser, smarter, and more incomprehensible than the automatic rifle bullets in the capital. The moon ridiculed me; the valley shivered, with little emotion. Smart dust motes of the size of a grain of sand contain sensors, computational capability, bidirectional wireless communication, and a power supply, and are inexpensive enough to be deployed by tens of millions. The torn pages fluttered to the north, leaving the atomized cities behind. The deranged caravan of a million sacked assumptions staggered to the south, skirting pulverized villages. Smart dust motes with applications in weather/seismological monitoring, chemical/biological sensors, weapons stockpile monitoring, and defense-related sensor networks. Is smart dust stardust carrying messages from Mars?

The headset of my portable radio repeated again and again

dust is also Buddha.

The ground war is declared over but not the dust. The order is collected but not the dust. He said, *How many have you counted. How did they fall?* Dust rises in spirals, airborne, everywhere.

Buddha = no answer.

Say something. Will you say something?

In the distance unfolds the demise of the Silicon Valley. Driven by Schrödinger's cat, Schopenhauer's will, and Siddhartha's belly. In the distance beckons the embryo of quantum computing to crack encrypted messages in the dust.

> *Dear S:*
> *Are you the secret agents for the operation oil change distributed*
> *at every gas station in the Death Valley or of the spreading disease*
> *claiming thousands of camels' lives or from the inferior enemy States*

for classified information of anthrax-based bio-weapons or from the publishing amalgamation running to full capacity continuously turning out brand-new books of paper bills and metal coins with discrete face values which fill the forbidden band gaps in the capital crystal where no free electrons are ever permitted?

SHE: Are you there, A?

Yes, I say, Scandinavia. I shudder and calm down.

Work nano, think cosmologic. That is to think of P. Together P and I became PIs (Principal Investigators) of all up-and-coming stars and upsets in major tournaments around the globe, to resolve our often conflicting predictions and inclinations, and PIs (Private Investigators) of every stroke of each eccentric off-court anecdote of world-class players, as if to scout leads to masterful executions at the table, as if to determine parameters of hidden terms in our interatomic potential energy.

Together P and I were called Pipi in the Ping-Pong circuit, since we always practiced together and played doubles as a pair in every tournament we entered. Together P and I operated the most comprehensive table tennis website in the world, with a IP (Internet Protocol) of 31.41.59.2, a website of circular loop, in which P renormalized, naturalized, nominalized, and indexed all circumferential singular inquiries about the Ethiopian spin in the upper half loop, and in which I designed, fabricated, and presented diametrical answers in the lower half, a website with a chatroom that was flooded and jammed during every World Championship and Olympic Games, with live scores and on-line rooting and comments from fanatics and groupies.

Nice push. Spank it, baby. Come on. What an inside-out loop drive. Damn. Great block. Unbelievable. Push gently. Jia You (more oil). Serve short. Concentrate on the 3rd ball attack. Eat me. Drive deep to the middle. God. Turn over. Rub it more. Yes. Don't stop.

Heated words spun around so many different linguistic axes, from Albania, Algeria, America, Andorra, Angola, Argentina, Armenia, Austria, and Australia, words of such opposing views and invocations that they begot a recurring internet bug, which eventually shut down the chatroom and the website.

With their falling through, our Ping-Pong career buckled too, so did our rubbery relationship.

P said, Dubious roses keep knocking at my Window 2000 operating system from his keyboard, please advise me *how*. It was followed by infinite silence. Him, whom I must have seen in the Ion House. In silence I wondered what his atomic number was. My hideous silence in another dark night, which was only broken by the waiter's *We've run out of Soul on Today's Special, would you like another entry?* We departed without eating at all, and parted saying nothing to each other.

I changed rubbers and lost my feeling, she had admitted. Because of her sudden obsession with rackets covered by spongeless rubber with long spineless pimples outward, like forests of synthetic rubber birch, to annul the opponent's spin, instead of the regular sandwiched sponged smooth rubber with pimples inwards for the modernist topspin play, as if she had given up on stimulating and manipulating the rubbery flesh after years' frustration with her inability to contain the senseless spin with the blood-sponged rubber surface rubbing against the celluloid ball, or because of the capillary attraction and/or distraction of posing brain pimps dressed as leggy bare-butt supermodels striding the fashion show runway of the postmodern poetic T stage, or her new passion for the single syllable *da* or its double *dada* in sitting meditation instead of the elusive friction coefficient μ between rubber and celluloid lubricated by the melodic streams of *Fantasia Impromptu*, or her disillusion with my tangential answers to or dodging all together her gothic perpendicular probing *would you push deep to my forehead if I couldn't make the backhand loop.*

SHE: Is it too short?

Like a quantum dot, which has no practical application in the foreseeable future, I knead, I pull, I plunge and bury my tongue in a smooth thrust into the warm wet inwards of the potential well V. Screw the present, scroll the past, and scrape the future. I have no concubines in any tense of time.

By degrees the opening angle increases.

M . . . o . . . o . . . r, she moans intermittently.

At the fundamental frequency of the palace of extreme pleasures. Like the fitful shouts and prayers from the unbroken line of parades on the boulevard in its never arriving march to the imperial palace.

In the friction trace there is small structure nested within large structure, which appears to be self-similar, and the friction force builds smoothly but drops abruptly and breaks time-reversal symmetry.

There's no turning back. How I treasure this refurbished room that provides adequate space for freedom of movement, of the stiffened abrasive tongue, after forever darting sideways in the cold, the cold of speech outside the covers of the book. What it meant to be out of doors in all weathers. What did I do to get here? How did I get here? No train ever arrives at this station. I am not holding it back, I am not holding this tongue, for god's sake. My last lodging in this random house. This bird nest. Like in the song. *Three times daily.* My stray legs forgot the long road the moment she opened the back door for me. I had long since lost the old room number, or it had never occurred to me at all, let alone its fantastic name. The room of all rooms.

Even swarms of worms bang iambically against the front door, shouting *let me in* or *let me out*. Either way. Never linger more than a second between *in* and *out*. As if an Archimedean ghost hiding in-between tilted the lever of the permanent gradient of longings or desperations to the *in* side or the *out* side never passing the equilibrium position ȯr ñeḭther ḭṅ ṅȯṭ ȯuṭ ȯr both *in* and *out*. To bend the eigenvectors of the 1st person 3rd world story of negatively charged electron worms away from the systematically renovated ancient city wall, from the stone wall of the imperial palace, from the extension of the fragmented Great Wall, from the post-postmodern wall of 2nd-rate 2nd-hand 3rd-person linear narration?

> *Dear S:*
>
> *Are you the story of the 2nd person or merely parody of the self? Are*
>
> *you the 2nd-order hyperbolic PDE governing non-Fourier heat flow*
>
> *with incomplete boundary conditions and indeterminable initial*
>
> *conditions or the 2nd-order strain tensor in the text of a stranger*
>
> *looking for an imaginary normal to act on?*

Write involutely (from circularly defined words); live straight.

Animal scent burns into my fingers, displacing smells of disinfectants, soaps, lotions, baby oils, plastic flowers, candles, rubber boots, rubber gloves, and rubber sheaths. Rabbit or duck? Headache. Tight room, loose thoughts. Story of the interference fit. What happens outside the room counts for nothing.

A . . . e. . . i . . . o . . . u, she vowels rhythmically.

The frequency-quadrupled sound permeates the entire room after multiple reflections, superimposing as another harmonic on the ongoing melody of *Camel Fantasia.* The dissipation mechanism of fluctuations in friction force must involve coherent dissipative structures that extend over distances that are huge compared with molecular dimensions because, if they did not, they would average out over the vastly large dimension of the samples, which are the metallic violin string, the room, the valley, the story.

SHE: Room!

There's no room on the moon. And there is no moon in the room either. I mean it literally. Fruitlessly I strived to pull the vault of heaven down onto the valley for the eigenvalues of my 1st story. Instead I relished my old wounds, my triangular wounds migrating from head to toe and back to head again.

High-ceiling machine shops rattling with metallic voices ranging a mile-long spectrum in which no human speeches could be identified, from motors, bearings, shafts, from red-hot chips curling off workpieces and entangling cutting tools, even from the very foundation that houses the machines. The random vibrations of *Firmiana simplex* tree leaves never ceased despite the wishes of its roots. Each machine with its unique fundamental modes of screech, be it hydraulic press, mechanical press, lathe, drill press, or milling machine, for whatever workpiece material and size, whether it is manually operated or computer-controlled, at whatever hour of the day. What did the machines try to say? Vibration- temperature- and humidity-controlled metrology laboratories permeated with machine oil smells in which K and I had to repeat in odd hours our assigned experiments that had gone wrong every time. Tiered classrooms occupied and deserted day in day out by anonymous intersections or interlocutions of regionally accented tongues behind outdated textbooks in the back rows. The cold huge walled-in outdoor cinema square where we were mesmerized by *The Yellow Earth*. The hot indoor auditorium where each line of the speeches was bent by soaked letters and thoroughly washed heads beginning with every letter, K, X, and I among them.

The discreteness of energy states of the story is determined by the finiteness of the dimension and size and potential energy of the room in which it unfolds.

142 steps from the portal to the top story, I counted as she guided me in along the spiral.

Is there a 4th person narration?

The room grows larger and brighter. More clearance for the imagination. More energy levels for the story. With increasing angular momentum. My vertex touches the bottom. Is there a different atom? The angle opens up to 60° then stops, while a horizontal bar is rising rapidly from the bottom of the V. Rabbit or duck. I see a ∀.

For all the words I loved before. Then nothing. Nothing can turn the V into a ∇, the gradient at narrative discontinuities, and therefore Δ, which measures the tendency of narrative gradient to converge upon a given point of view. Δ, the discriminant to determine the behavior of solutions of systems of algebraic equations of the tuple (K, X, I) with real coefficients a_i. Yet something mutates restlessly below this bottomless bottom. It is a peanut. No, a pretzel. No, a bitter melon. The inseparable tri-colored triplet of two up quarks and one down quark forms the proton, with superstrings at their heart. The protocol of the formation of the merry-go-round ring of proto-wounds of being. The prototype of the protagonist's 1st coming. Coming out of space, into space. Coming of age. The Iron Age. The age of irony.

I did not come. I simply entered.

You never enter the text via the front door in any perverted composition.

They entered the besieged capital. Alas. The mechanized animals. They came. They are coming again.

> *Dearest S:*
>
> *Are you slow too slow in coming? Are you too short too short of breath*
> *too short of here and now?*

Not being let into the circular master bedroom of the pink St. Ring the dejected worms were turned away from the locked front door into the curved hallway by magnetic flux. The delivery boy still rings the doorbell in strings of consonants. It starts contracting with urgency.

SHE: Faster, fascist Animal!

The roaring steam from her body rocks my train of thought to Berlin. I breathe and sweat heavily to maintain the *prestissimo* pace of my arm, and my conversation with old masters. Rilke wrote, True singing is a different breath, about nothing. You show me the feel of nothing. I feel I pluck the A string.

SHE: Oh, A++!

My thought is back to the Time(s) Square.

With four eyes wide open, with portable computerized CMM (Coordinate Measurement Machine), excited by the prospect of squared time, I kissed, I gawked, I crept and crawled from dawn around every square inch of the mapped locality of the Times Square, for an area which would approximate the Time Square, or simply any square, my bare belly squeaking *time time time time* in each direction, on the burning marble sideways, on the asphalt walkways for Xing. *Time* won't tell squarely. Until I was swamped again by the T storm at high noon. Thick smoke of burnt birds and fury of falling leaves in the capital had migrated by natural convection or abnormal solar wind of the sextet sun, but was instantly crystallized by the afterfreezer of the still-fresh violent hours, which in turn was turned into the crucible of infinite duration of forgetting to heal the cracks in the goblet holding cherry-flavored red wine of our bared emotions—we stripped their thick outfit inherited from ancestors, sages and legends, emperors and dynasties—the crucible to restore permanent deformations in our soul by monstrous blows, the crucible to vaporize out of the giant crystal ball of reverie all impurities of memory, which are incompatible with abstract musing and inherently light-weighted because they are embedded in a honeycomb structure. The crucible plagued by un-catalogued mechanical malfunctions.

I realize that all the time I spent is locked in a three-way knot formed by three extensive axes, along which propagate waves of caravans indexed as 7, 35, and 140 respectively, none of which can be obtained by squaring a rational number, and which by a stretch of imagination could form a disintegrated right triangle, if their lengths satisfy Pythagoras' theorem. Could Pythagoras have foreseen a right triangle with the transfinite relationship $\infty^2 + \infty^2 = \infty^2$ since $7^2 + 35^2 < 140^2$? Or time diverges in three different directions on the same plane from the common intersection point, which is the abstraction of the platform of the ancient train station, which however is by no means the origin of time. Squared amplitude of the time-dependent wave function = probability of the position of Time Square. But how to measure? *Time* never tells. Time Square is another delusion. I would never again speculate about the squareness of time. I would never again try to square time, even though I am confined in the square potential well of the imperial city.

Dear S:

Are you the tenderized saga of the evolution of city waste or the frozen samba? Are you the black sound of Time Square or the logarithmic scale of the slide rule with a base of ear?

ɪ: Are you there, Scandinavia?

SHE: Yeah, I am arriving, on the divine spaceship through a through hole in the liquefied ozone layer from the moon, Saint Augustine.

She jumps off the periodic table onto the floor. The strings unwind. The music stops abruptly. But not my listening. Not again after years of deaf-muteness to the resonance of forbidden pleasures.

She unlocks the door.

ɪ: Scandinavia, stand still, don't move a muscle.

SHE: What are you doing, A?

ɪ: Nothing, just looking.

An inverse isosceles triangle with two cherry petal vertices swirling on twin silicone half domes like flowers of deadly infectious disease, and an oasis of potential well, a wellspring 100-years deep rippling across desert dunes. One center, two guards. The hirsute sun, guarded by global laws describing elliptic orbits of its four nearest moons and local criteria of opening up doors to different interpretations of the laws. The positive ∇ reconstructed from the lost Si out of the V cleavage by wet and anisotropic chemical etching. The abstract expressionist painting held steady by its own beauty of the intrinsic geometrical form of manifolds. Why can we only sense three spatial dimensions? $\overset{\cdot}{K}, X^m, I_2$. Two charm quarks and one strange quark spin at the speed of light. Where is the 4th person?

SHE: Just looking? Liar. What are you thinking, bad Air?

I don't look away. I am not afraid of such pleasures anymore. I don't know how to look beyond the front view. I had looked away all my life until yesterday when I received as a surprising birthday present new glasses with UV filter coating to alleviate my failing eyesight aggravated daily by the triply magnified adjective sun: *great, glorious, righteous.*

> *Dear S:*
>
> *Are you the stripper in the feast of poetry in the National*
>
> *Poetry Month?*

Under the hottest sun in four decades I_2 was born in the capital on the shiny June night as a miracle son of the winter, after 40 year-old widowed ma was kissed once on the right side of her skull by a missionary nun from the snow mountain to quench the rampant 750°C fever that had brought her down. A birth express. An **M** transformation which, involving only a complicated shearing process of the γ lattice, is diffusionless and therefore time-independent. A child prodigy in deep and useless thoughts but a retard in speech and other bodily functions. Thought has since been my singular aptitude, my only affect. For a time I thought I was another kind. A sphere of head and body in one, a sphere nested in another, concentric, metallic, separated by a cm-wide gap, to detect gravitational waves produced by violent events in the distant universe. A spherical harmonic of *seen* and *unseen* with parameters (0, 0). A spherical joint with sockets of varying shapes, sizes and depths, asymmetrically distributed on the surface, with little hands and feet and thin long limbs dangling listlessly. It must be. A

spherical aberration soon to haunt the objective lens in the Hubble Space Telescope, whose diagnosis by NASA evoked my 1st awareness of my spherical existence.

I_3 looks on. I look on through all the thickness of my new glasses. *Twilight - flooding eloquence - fairy cave.* The perfect source of synchrotron orbital radiation. Of the X-ray bundle with a critical wavelength of 1Å and a cone opening of 0.2 mrad. You can definitely look and think at the same time.

Dear ma, I can't blame your 20/20 for my poor vision. Too much secret reading with too little understanding.

I'm reading with total absorption, therefore absolutely with no reflection. Murderous twin *Heights* hangs onto *robotic birch*. One reads *Hamiltonian,* the other *Himalayas.* One reads *Histogram,* the other *Hum.* Then both read $\hbar$.

My 1st reading. My 1st exposure to the hard X-rays. My 1st reading with ousted poets at midnight in the basement of the Empire Building.

> *Dearest S:*
>
> *Are you stomach-ly flat?*

The best sphericity is that of the neutron star. The μm spherical particles found among grinding chips indicate occurrence of melting during the grinding process. The unthinkable cm single teardrop on father's cheek when he faced me at the door after my getaway was almost a liquid sphere.

Fear is spherical.

Topologically a cube, a cylinder, and a sphere are equivalent objects.

SHE: Tell me more, please, please.

For (10-1) years I_1 blindly beat waist drums in the grand *campaign of four-wheel drive* orchestrated by the tacit new emperor, who had been fed up with sight of a nation of bicycles, into the *open door* of the national dancehall still in its long overdue overhaul, sang *wine and coffee and song* en route to classrooms, and barely missed, seeking the 5th wheel in the unmanned humanity private parts of the library abused by technical texts, the inscrutable virus of *spiritual contamination*, under which the emperor labeled all the buzzing insects and pollen of sexless love prying into the imperial ballroom, as if they would have thwarted his hypersexual imperial drive. I_1 indulged, while chasing nonstop all conceivable conceptual and concrete aspects of the production of steel parts and the ultimate mother machine which makes and spooks all machines, *freedom of logogram* in the *congregation*, until my 1st violent and instant death, and yet was born again, thanks to medical advancement carried ashore by the 3rd wave of industrial revolution, as I_2, out of the dead I_1 from the emergency room packed with other mothers and stillborns after the catastrophe, I_2 still suffering from *post-cesarean section* and *post-heat treatment* symptoms.

Pieces of June broken from steel and steel-reinforced concrete.

> *Dearest S:*
>
> *Are you the supersaturated solid-solution of poetry in fiction?*

The 2.73°K cosmological wind hisses in B-flat through bassoon, clarinet, flute, and oboe, from every direction. The dripping Rilke, 6 in. tall, 2 in. wide, and 1 in. thick, creeps out of the blue. Out of the cleavage of words. For a fleeting moment I hear the true singing.

This hiss vexes me.

Dear ma, can you tell me again the title of the song in the vector field of hope near the cave?

Two unconventional methods to make holes in the steel ball are by electron beam and laser.

Common to these processes are highly localized deliveries of high-energy beams, high drilling rates, easy automation, high-capital investment, and unavoidable thermal damage to the surrounding material.

Your proof of the existence of U in the sphere of SiO_2 contains a huge fat hole. Your proof of the theorem that towers are precipitated mountains, and therefore must form spontaneously in the desert, contains a network of the huge hollow paper moons of Ali Baba.

For an unproven proposition in any axiomatic system, there is absolutely no way of ascertaining whether its proof is impossible or simply very difficult within the axioms of the system. What's more, to prove the consistency of that system, one must go beyond it.

Where were the enemies? Where are the enemies of now of now of now?

Any kind of crime is admitted in mahogany as long as you are not ashamed to play and can pay.

Reader, please forward me hoodwinking recipes to make computer-unreadable holes.

The world is upside-down; the world is the mirror image of my wounds. The sacred world. Two up quarks and one down quark spin clockwise and counter-

clockwise at the same time. K, X, and I. *When we meet again after 20 years* . . . .
What's the definitive name of the 4th person? Toward the apex of the inversed white
mountain my wandering thought strives to home again. Why are there only three
families of fermions?

With no additional charge, she lets me inspect the interior of her imperative supreme
cunt with the signifier glass.

SHE: Come eat me. Eat my cone.

Inside the Secretary is giving another head to the head of the State over the net of
the Ping-Pong table in the veranda, as the emperor sinking deep into the armchair
on the hearth looks on with that eternal fatherly smile philosophizing the new word
order. Inside the vast empty ballroom of the expanding imperial palace.

Fuck 2nd-order elliptic PDEs of the governing laws of static States. Fuck 2nd-order
inhomogeneous hyperbolic PDEs with extreme perturbations from aggressive States.
Fuck indeterminate initial conditions.
Fuck boundary conditions of the 1st kind.
Fuck boundary conditions of the 2nd kind.
Fuck boundary conditions of the 3rd kind.
Fuck periodic boundary conditions.
Fucking moving boundary conditions.

On the wide-stretched lime wall are glossy microchips, glittering in a
pattern of approximately 2.57 rainbows *Made in No-Man's-Land with illegally-
acquired technologies.*

Do you love me amanita?

Do you love me ambrosia?

Do you love me ambarella?

Do you love me amboyna?

Do you love me amsincknia?

Do you love me amoeba?

Do you love me amphisbaena?

Do you love me ammonia?

Do you love me amenorrhea?

Do you love me amyotonia?

Do you love me amblyopia?

Do you love me ametropia?

Do you love me amentia?

Do you love me amnesia?

Do you love me amygdala?

Do you love me amphora?

Do you love me ampulla?

Do you love me amrita?

SHE: Would you vote me, *Counter?*

Inside the V cleavage inflate moist folds of my tubular wounds inside which streams of my memory bursts with breathless vacuum energy. With my absent superpartners: $\widetilde{K}, \widetilde{X}, \widetilde{I}$.

Can't. Can't. Can't. (Repeat 18 times.)

Drink the water, she commands.

Where is it from, Madam *Mad Am*, I am lost again.

SHE: Any bottles that are open.

The unresolved paradox of information loss in the interior of the black hole.

The day before yesterday I saw $\dot{K}$ and I_3 acting *Madam Butterfly* to the delight of X'' as they watched goldfish jumping above the surface of the man-made lake, then heard X' tell $\ddot{K}$ and I_2 the 3rd story from the snow mountain, among chirping birds which had returned overnight from overseas and converged to the lake on this 8th day of April, while drowning ourselves in *The Diving Girl*, which was plunging into the ocean from the campus radio station, a melody which however goes on in my head, one day in the forehead, another in the back head, one day in the left head, another in the right head, and reaching out for petals of the dying numbers 8s, 9s, 1s, undocumented, unemployed, undressed, sexless, dimensionless, countless, when I strayed alone to gather scattered cherry petals in my dream. The cherry petals conversed, danced in the air with the air in each blossoming April of the ancient city, then cascaded into the lake in front of the main library, into the buzzing fountain in the center of the square lotus pond in the deepest water of the lake, quickly converting the lake the lotus pond and the fountain into the cherry lake the cherry pond and the cherry fountain, then shot up back into the air from the fountain the pond the lake before falling back again, the soaked cherry petals, we are talking about the cherry, and migrated, after a whole week of frantic reciprocal motion, with purple of April pink of April violet of April mauve of April lavender of April albumen of April albescence of April albino of April chalk of April fair of April ferrite of April hoary of April lactescence of April pale of April snow of April, in uncertain steps, one by one, in Indian file, to the concave campus gate, the orifice of the knowledge lake, towards the unknown, as if unaccustomed to the sudden bend of direction of motion by the horizontal wind, or dragged by the viscous water, nevertheless were driven by the rapidly shrinking and bifurcating field of multi-phase horizontal flow, and finally disappeared into the labyrinth of world pipes.

SHE: Blue field, another optical illusion in artificial light.

Last night without glasses on, I somnambulated out of the tightly guarded apartment to find the sweet spot in the moon. Through dark streets and desolate fields in the abstract landscape which must still be under curfew, X'' and I_3 eagerly engraved my cheek, that is, my belly, my forehead, that is, my chest, and my lips, that is, my labia; silently $\dot{K}$ and I_2 reflexed the mysterious bow singing *when we meet again in 20 years, who will be the one to toast to?* I circled and circled the apartment complex in vain, until I turned the corner of the 21st century when the moon jumped right on my face. The brightness of the moonlight blinded my naked eyes because they had never been accustomed to the closeness and roundness of the glowing yellow whole, while my hand was blindly feeling the peaks and valleys on the moon surface with the revolver. Convinced that it must be the ghostly sun with a cold yellow shield I shot it three times and it was gone for good from my life.

The one-pointed arrow of love, sheer fiction, the head is blunt, the arrow wet, she hisses again.

The dead march toward me. In different versions. In different orders of time derivatives and spatial derivatives. At different velocities, accelerations, and jerks. From different points, slopes, and curvatures. $\mathbf{K} = [\,K, \dot{K}, \ddot{K}, \dddot{K}, \ldots\,]$, $\mathbf{X} = \quad X, X', X'', X''', \ldots\,]$, and $\mathbf{I} = [\,I_0, I_1, I_2, I_3, \ldots\,]$. Three free vectors perpetually pointing at the adrift me as if proposing scalar toasts *have we melted* with vectorial gazes.

You examine me. You shoot at me.

May I stay a little longer, just a little longer, till the rain is over?

SHE: Your time is up. Get up. Be a man and assume a convex attitude.

When will we meet again?

Three times my index finger pulls the trigger. This is not the triple assassination I plotted therefore ever committed. Only intent counts. What is the intent of this text? Results are beyond devil's dream. I let 100 roses bloom in the body-scape of murderous rapture. Four months after the massacre was celebrated the golden wedding of the emperor in the barricaded Square, which was thronged with flowers of all colors from around the country in place of the cheering teens. I read 0 strain from the roseate Wheastone Bridge Circuit instantly bonded on her forehead, chest, and buttoned belly. I record anomaly of high iron in the red-hot blood streams.

The probability fog across the SiO_2 Bridge and around the Empire Building never disperses.

With my magic bow I painstakingly bandsaw her head off, as if playing the A note of the mourning tune on a double bass, and bury it deep inside her blown up cunt. I look into it again and am stunned by disappearing masked heads, my own heads with plastered labels, in no particular order, e.g., *a lyric poet who never writes a poem, a novelist who can't read novels, a law-biding citizen who is constantly on the run from the law, a die-hard utopist who has no clue about the true character of U—the union of A and Z, or the unitary operator on the hyperspace, or . . . ?*

Dead. Dead. Dead. Dead.

No need for head. A period will do.

Deep inside her closing cunt are buried balls of all sorts: a soccer ball labeled as *logic bomb*; a meatball which cheers *mis-isms*; an apple ball whispering *annihilate your ex-*

accomplice; a cannonball screaming *almighty din*; a Ping-Pong ball spinning *friction of epistemology*; a ball bearing ball which hails *to the axial vector*; a basketball tainted with the spit of *pubic fervor*.

Balls. All balls.

No more spheroidization. No more theorization. No more fictionalization.

My feet recite *that which died is affirmed and thus must have been* while wiping clean the scarlet cleavage in the deflating whole with my waterproof index finger, and zip it up with crazy gluon.

To be buried in Sweden.

The dead never die. They built a Shangri-La in the Death Valley in my heartland where 1,000 birds sing *May Day May Day* under the gibberish sun. I hear again the orange sirens. I smell shark sashimi with wasabi sauce and egg drop broth. There's no Amitabha in the upscale brothel. There's no Amitabha in the asylum for the tormented spirit. The message is in the alphabet bathtub. The message was the world-encapsulated dust, translated scattered and disrobed.

> *Dearest S:*
>
> *I am not inquiring about your history. We will never see each other again. Meet me between would-be stations. Love from the Panic Station. A.*

Three billion eggs come and go every month. I am not cooking them all up. Pairs of quarks and anti-quarks wink in and out of existence constantly in Geneva. Every second hundreds of billions of nutrinos stream through our bodies screaming *thou thou*, never heard, never felt. Bitstreams of *0*s and *1*s power through networks of undersea optical fibers at terahertz frequency, never forming the identity matrix *I*. The sweating heads rub off each other in job fairs at the Saint Clara Convention Center for a vacancy in dotcoms. Words arrive in triangles and squares and leave in circles without any lasting registration in the brain. However my wounds just stay. They never came. I never let them go. My abstract wounds with no definite shapes and locations.

The Mexican boy drops the $4.95 Japanese lunch special, hurries out of the flowering room without payment. I am always thirsty. *Forget me not*, her record player spins my ass out of the rear door into the UV rays of the setting sun in the rain. The fortune cookie squeaks

change your blue jeans into the crimson robe at 36.

I'm a black bird, she hums again.

Dark energy. White momentum. Gray matters of the brain. Gray interior of the A train. The Andromeda spirals away at ever-increasing angular velocity. What an abstracted afternoon.

Out of her ruby cavern, out of the blind hole, 1 inch toward the Empire Building through the rain, my confidence riding high on the convexity of the old man's pointed remarks. Yet my body of positive photoresist has been unable to *selectively* absorb the hard X-ray radiation, therefore my each colorblind high-aspect ratio wound resists any curing, more than that, it deepens and metamorphoses after each direct contact with the 4-D spacetime, thriving with a life of its own, with its exotic anatomies diffracted by the incidental X-ray:

A moving trihedron.

A lead bullet ball buried in the buttock.

A French curve in T-squares.

An army of anemia policing every blood cell.

A stream of AIDS (Acquired Identity-Deficiency Syndrome) drowning every impulse of the intentionality of language.

A ring of 40 mm-sized laser-drilled holes in the heart muscle (a chest pain relief operation approved by FDA in 1998).

A 3.5 floppy drive A: dismayed at the constipated self storage.

An A surfacing from time to time above the ocean of THEs in the incontinent bladder.

Dearest S:

What's your real name, not the email alias? Sabina, Swan, Shanghai, sangha, Santa, silly man, standard deviation, Standard Model, squark, stereo-lithography, or shuttle to Time Square? Or simply somebody something somewhere somehow someway sometime out of anybody anything anywhere anyhow anyway anytime?

It says, *Give me a trillion, I will open one puffy eye.*

It says, *Give me a googol, I will cry out once.*

His hairs fly high in the air like columnar snowflakes under the glowing stage light. Snow never falls on this mirage stage. Amazingly the reading is still on even though I'm hours behind schedule. His gold words radiate brilliant energy into my navel, with unheard clarity and transparency, *You can use the word . . . W - O - U - N - D . . . in your - poems - only once - in your lifetime . . . everything - must be - concrete . . . photographic images, no abstract words, no freedom, no truth, no justice, no soul, no heart, no love.* But I never claimed my dozen reels of developed film negatives, fearing the worst yet to develop in the already exposed worsened wounds. But my wounds have never been singular as shown by the X-ray images, and I can't spell any one without mentioning all of them at once. I ransack papers, manuscripts, condoms, and bottles in my knapsack for my *American Heritage,* for my revolver, only to find my magic bow.

I hear a quiet crunch.

My life as an electron-stripped composite atom.

I am positive. With a positive charge of +459. A dense ensemble of totally ionized atoms: noble gas Ar (Argon), or my breath, nonmetals As (Arsenic), At (Astatine), or my memory, rare earth metals Ac (Actinium), Am (Americium), or my blood, and transitional metals Ag (Silver), Au (Gold), Al (Aluminum), or my butt-length mane.

$A = \sum_i A_i$, where $i = c, g, l, m, r, s, t, u$.

A substitutional point defect in the α grain in the partially transformed **P**.

Yet still an incomplete set. Where did the missing indices go?

Not silicon. Not Si again.

Not again this '90s chic this techie cult this Wall Street icon this ambiguous character in the Ion House. Because the pseudo proximity between S and i in the periodic table can never close the widening gap between S and I. I'd had my uneventful affair with the rich Si and bid my farewell to it, because it, seated comfortably between Al and P on the same story in the periodic table, being transferred repeatedly like the veiled bride in-between diffusion furnaces, resist spinners, steppers, resist developers and strippers, wet and dry etchers, deposition stations, and ion implanters in the clean room, with total steps well over hundreds for a typical chip, yet unable to emit any visible light, has betrayed the sands anchoring from time immemorial at the intersection of land and sea, and blindly powers the dotcom frenzy and deluges of concrete misinformation, and therefore drowns the true singing.

Is there an alternative story consistent with SiO_2? Si as a mechanical material as a new medium for *direct writing*?

I don't live in Livermore no more. Not I.

But all atoms together only account for about 5% of this flat universe. This is not science fiction.

The universe is a stretching sheet of black rubber whitened sporadically with trillions of letter S, inverted.

Before succumbing to this degenerate matter my breasts glimpse through the half-above-the-ground windows, and I'm bedeviled by a very concrete ongoing poetic wrestling on the concrete floor, a concrete simultaneous cardinal triangulation or ordinal strangulation for the fat whole in the head, or the flat hole in the bottom, under the concrete roof of this modernist concrete building: Ginsberg's esoteric argon and pious tone mixed with street talk are all over Mayakovsky and Bachaman, Duncan and Pessoa are teasing Weiner with senseless similes and outrageous metaphors, Khlebnikov is throwing new flaws of humanity to Lautréamont and Lu Xun, Stein and Hölderlin are tingling recklessly Vallejo with reclusive verbs, Shi Zhi (Index Finger) is fingering Bernhard and Artaud turning classless nouns to the noble rank of verbs.

SHI ZHI: This is the capital at 4:30 AM, tides of heads ebbing; this is the capital at 4:30 AM, all lights screaming at once.

GINSBERG: Fainting on the laptop with a vision of ultimate loop.

BERNHARD: Inside the tiny cone design the gigantic spherical shell as the adobe for all the displaced imported zoo-ed giant pandas in the capital and cities around the globe, outside their home forest south to the ancient city, to satisfy the curiosity of the masses. Build it in the very center of the forest of the national park.

ARTAUD: For the children of the Lagrangian of the world are not in the grunt but in the cunt, which isn't the subtle correlations of the law but an ultimate conspiracy. Not in the cone but in the cunt, extreme convulsion which campaigns hard with its loops, to swallow up all beings.

MAYAKOVSKY: Thus to all inflation theories.

LAUTRÉAMONT: That night, we, that is, dogs, cats, chickens, and rabbits, in a rowdy party in the basement kitchen of the big house in the center of the forest, to celebrate my return, prepared poisoned spicy soup in the melting pot. Two dogs brought in a black goat and dropped it into the pot, while it was splashing and bleating in the frothing scum, everyone else cheered and shouted hilariously, "Traitor! Traitor!" Goats, coats with no felt gratitude to the law.

LU XUN: The past death is alive. I'm saddened by this aliveness, because through it I know it has not been. The living dead is flowering. I'm saddened by this floweringness, because from it I know it has been emptiness.

BACHAMAN: It was mass spectrometer.

WEINER: A forbidden sentence almost makes sense without microstructure-like middle.

BACHAMAN: It was mass.

BERHARD: Appropriate the plot to install the ball in the middle of the forest.

BACHAMAN: Specter.

MAYAKOVSKY: Hunt the Higgs boson.

LAUTRÉAMONT: At 4:30 AM I woke up with a searing pain in the butt. Four black goats were holding each leg, while the 5th was thrusting his horn in and out of me, and all were cursing, "this is the welcome you deserve, asshole!" In shock I had swallowed my own tongue, my head buried in the heap of my own muck.

HÖLDERLIN: What is poetry for?

BERNHARD: All books, drawings, materials, machines about the making of the massive ball.

LU XUN: Science, science, in science perishes that which can't be proved scientifically.

KHLEBNIKOV: Here's another proof of Positive Mass Theorem.

BERNHARD: Leave, leave behind this machinery this system, and the sooner a man of intellect turns his back on this machinery, this system, the better.

MAYAKOVSKY: Long live the 3rd superstring revolution!

DUNCAN: Unbend the rainbow with ultra-fast UV laser.

PESSOA: Spontaneous symmetry breaking: a left-handed violet square inner singular solution of the 100-year-old problem *there* and *then* corresponds by translation to the right-handed violent pentagonal outer general solution *here* and *now* in search of a problem.

BERNHARD: No more *ifs*. No matter what new fonts what new materials they are made of.

STEIN: Paths to Lake of Composition: come; pose; oppose; purpose; proposition; posit; position; deposit; impose; expose; depose; exposition; repose; reposit; reposition; transpose; superposition; juxtapose; dispose.

KHLEBNIKOV: I have corrected the fundamental flaws of time travel and now it will be as easy to predict events as to count the number of quantum states of a black hole. If you don't want to listen to my science of predicting past lives I shall announce it to giant pandas.

VALLEJO: My homecoming turned my home into a tomb. I bit ma to shreds with my fangs of ignorance, strangled the house lady with my forelegs of faked cuteness, crushed the cats with my paws, froze the rabbits' blood with my tungsten-framed bespectacled face, inflicted fatal blows to fellow dogs with my poisoning saliva, and seduced the mad dogs with my pastoral tunes to swallow the goats. I was reborn as a mad dog that dawn.

LU XUN: I have only my elegy to escort Z to the platform, hoisted from my dynamic random-access memory. I will remember: for myself, and for again thinking of my escorting Z to the platform with my memory.

SHI ZHI: If I could, as a buggered robotic dog, break the merciless chain, I'll readily renounce the goddamn bill.

LU XUN: I'll set my left foot into the new millennium, I'll bury the truth with my right foot deep down inside the ancient wound in mother earth, my heart leaping and sinking in situ, guided by forgetting and lying.

SHI ZHI: Because this is my capital, because this is my last capital.

I awoke from the dream and saw the telegram again: *Pythagoras dying too. Return to cave ASAP.*

Among scarlet capes the old man is digging fiercely the lectern with plastic highlighters in both hands and banging his silvery head in the air without punctuation marks, muttering *fuck off with triangular inequality.*

There's not a single spectator at all, except a cordon along the wall. Among the background noises of axes chopping the network of roots of birch trees outside the building, are moaning, sighs, screaming, kicks, spanking, *nope - nay - nil - nix - non - nein - nyet - ν - mei - bu*, which constitute the 9th Symphony of Poetry, to which dances the absent 1st figure.

What are you reading tonight?

This is not the assumed reading scene. But I can't resist the temptation. Inside my empty stomach chorus of the multitude of deafening beats,

Spa/Ce . . . Cu/r(v)ed. Ti - me . . . m-eat-y. Go-d St-r(a)ight. St/or/y is ill-con-Ce-IV-ed is I-ll. W/or/LD is ne/it/her im-age no/r so/U/ND. Glob-Al pos/it/ion/in/g. Lo-Cal ex-T-re-mum. Boo/GI/e-woo/g/ie. W-or-d Ga-me. A/to/m trap/ping. S/pin/ ½. Circ/U/l/Ar pro/ton-pro/to/N col-lid-er. W/or/M/hole. LA/St tan-go on a tan-gent pl-an-e.

Where are they from? Where is the 4th person?

Befuddled, I am inducted as the makeshift conductor of the Poetry Whorehouse Orchestra in a 6-D torus compacted from the hidden extra dimensions, the unknown dimensions of humanity.

A huge flat screen of DLP (Digital Light Processing) projection system by TI is raster-scanning on the background of the stage:

POETRY AUCTION: THE LAST BID

Soup

Poetry with rime or numbers soup	Pt $1.50	Qt $3.00
Poetry with song soup	Pt $1.50	Qt $3.50

Appetizer

Fried poetry wings	$3.00
Steamed poetry dummies (6)	$3.75

Main entry

Poetry of fresh masquerade	$6.75
Poetry hooligan style	$6.75
Sweet and sour poetry	$6.75
Poetry on Mobius strip (w. 4 kicks, no rime)	$6.75
Poetry, story, and roast propaganda in black beast sauce	$7.50
Poetry of string beast	$7.50
Generation Z's poetry	$8.25
Oral poetry	$8.25
P.I.N. Poetry	$8.50
Syphilis poetry	$8.50
ASCII poetry	$8.50
Poetry with fresh bastard and garrison in chief's special X.O. sauce (Bastard delight)	$9.50
Skeletons & poetry sautéed w. militant Victorian in spicy brothel sauce (Triple delight)	$9.50
Poetry of logic	seasonal price
Poetry of lust	seasonal price

(P.S.: All proceeds go to the non-fiction collection of the Library of Congress.)

This is not fiction of science. Auditory and visual hallucinations are a hallmark of schizophrenia.

If I were to be born again, let me be a tope in Spain.
If if I were not to be born again, let me be a tope in Spain.
If if if I were neither to be born nor not to be born again, let me be a tope in Spain.

Down the devil's staircase I cleave the filthy air with my bow my baton, re-counting the number of steps. Through the revolving door, through the cordon, across the electrified room, I charge straight toward the cosmic background microwave radiation on the square stage with my manuscript.

Attention: This perverse composition and performance of poetry are to be dealt resolutely with by any means necessary, in observance of the Full Frontal Nude World Prose Year.

Is it the 4th person speaking? It's showtime anyway. A sphere turns into a spider. The net is broken. But I am too positive therefore already drifting farther away from my original story. In any case there would be no time for another story to unfold even if I figured out

the science of fiction.

No. It. C. If.

T SQUARE

The merit of originality is not novelty; it is sincerity.

—Peter Handke, *Kaspar and Other Plays*

You argue with me, among huddled crowd, my head gone, tongue dead, about metaphors of *asymptotic freedom* and undecidability of *past perfect truth*, and the facelift of the T Square, at its entrance on the boulevard.

The top view of the Square is a swelled and stretched T. Its pillar is swelled into a 5×5 mile square. On three sides it is sealed by glass walls; its 4th or north side, embraces, via a five-mile-long fence of barbed wire, the south side of the boulevard, a thick straight line extending both eastward and westward. A metal gate, built in the middle of the fence, stares squarely at the campanile in the center of the Square. A huge bronze bell has been installed atop the campanile, to replace the statue.

The Square, the capital within the capital.

As the gate opens and the Square unveils its new face, a SUV drives by like a spider, with a man and a woman in black straitjackets inside. Without warning they begin firing, 1st tear gas canisters, then rubber bullets, then exploding bullets, along with their anathema, *raw, red rum, live, live, live*, at anything on the boulevard. We run away in horror.

I find myself skating and skidding in the Square, like a hockey buck. I am the only one.

Where did they come from? How did they get through the State Security, the Public Security? Where are they heading?

The bell rings madly.

The Square surface is coated with carbon nanotubes. It's almost frictionless and thus wear resistant. It was designed to be the heaven's gate, eternal. On this holy plane, sliding is the only form of motion, and the only way to change direction is through impact against the wall. Straight line-segments are the only trajectories for any moving object on the perfectly flat surface. You slide like rays of geometric light, though not nearly as fast.

Until all your kinetic energy is absorbed by the walls, or, as a small-probability event, you escape the square trap and the street friction resumes the sanity of motion.

But I wear a pair of magnetic shoes that are driven by PZT actuators implanted in my glutei maximi and activated by a button on my waist belt, which can be switched off by excessive vibration of the body, such as that induced by the gas bursting out of the anus. The shoes enable me to suspend in the air and hold steady my position 0.1 in. above a steel surface and to fly with nanoresolution speed and trajectory control.

Yet my magnetic shoes are deactivated. I bounce between hard walls uncontrollably.

In the Pro-Engineer environment, I've animated a million possible routes traversing the Square, with different points of entrance and incident angles, to simulate our loitering in the Square in the daily festival when its concrete surface was being rapidly worn off by the nonstop stamping of spontaneously gathering and dispersing feet, to simulate optimal routes which both score most hits at the campanile and maximize my stay inside the Square. With a text box of the 15-min presentation inserted into the simulated Square. To share with you at the campanile.

In the Square I strive to aim at the campanile. In vain. I've lost my control button.

In the Square the air is filled with N_2 and He, with only 5% O_2; it is of the color purple, purple atoms of forgetting raining down incessantly from the square sky, purple molecules of remembering osmosing and vaporizing from earth, purple aerosols with a special hypnotizing effect. Subjects, hypnotized, freed from their exterior decency and interior fear, surrendered themselves readily to random intercourse with stranger objects. The purple inert air would force the crowd to move in and out of the Square at such a frequency that any seeds of wild ideas are kept from sustained interpenetration and fertilization and therefore the Square from litters, a great relief for the public health authority.

From *there* to *here* I have come such a long way by missing the T.

But I leave nothing to chance operation. I've equipped myself with an oxygen mask, and a shock-absorbing nanostructured greatcoat which resists diffusion of any kind through it. All invisible to normal human vision. We have finally materialized the cloth of the emperor.

My body skids and swirls, drawing incomplete triangles.

Din, xin, min, tai ying min, hai si tou, yelled Prof. Z, while he meant *dian, xian, mian, tou ying mian, hou shi tu,* in mandarin, or *point, line, plane, projection plane, rear view.* I listened hard harder and harder I listened but only got more lost after each listening in the rest of his unrecognizably accented words. Point to where? Along which line? On what plane? From whose point of view?

We were drawing on the A0 drawing papers projection lines, continuous and dashed, straight and curved, with our brand-new T-square, $30 \times 60 \times 90$ and $45 \times 45 \times 90$ degree triangles, a set of three compasses, French curve, and pencils from type H to HB to B and in that order.

I perpetually confused a continuous projection line with a dashed one of the projected object. I was never able to visualize its invisible external features and hidden internal ones; I was never able to construct their relations to its visible external features.

What was the actual machine we tried to design? A subassembly of the futuristic vehicle?

I drew extension lines, thin straight lines extending from each projection line in every orthographic view. Lines extended off margins around the front, side, and top views, off edges of the drawing board, passing through classroom walls, campus walls, and the thick ancient city walls, to join telecommunication cable, high-voltage cable of power grids, and rails of the nation's railway network. How could they extend their straightness all the way?

I drew double-arrowed dimensioning lines perpendicular to and bounded by arrow-free extension lines and wrote down numbers alongside them. Rational numbers to represent unambiguously and without redundancy the dimensions and tolerances of the object.

The intersected and interlocked projection extension dimensioning lines blotched the three views and quickly lost me. They made interpreting my design an impossible task, let alone throwing it over to the manufacturing line to the assembly line. They formed a wire-frame model of the prison cell for my temporal flirtation. Lines made of words *projections of 3-D mechanical hell.*

From then on I was never able to grasp a poetic line.

But I miss my T-square. I miss my plexiglas T-square coated with cherry scent.

More than once Prof. Z warned us, *Listen to me carefully, you there, or get an F.*

A huge crack opens up on the surface of the T Square and I fall right through it.

I fall away from IT. I fall away from IF IT IS.

I fall parabolically down the negative Z-axis, hearing the gate shut behind me. I fall into an abyss unfeeling my own weight.

I fall from EITHER.

With my fall fell short my fantasy about the return, the insane surface sliding, and my belated re-investigation.

My fall. Not my folly. The crack is not my folly. It must be the dogged working of the monstrous residual stresses in the surface, accumulated through many discrete manufacturing steps involved in its shaping through years, through rapid cycles of surface temperature fluctuations after that, like the fickle kinky appetites of the emperor, because the surface is made of multi-layers of drastically dissimilar materials, e.g., rock, soil, concrete, stainless steel, and carbon, from the bottom up. From the bottom I roll my eyeballs up and catch a glimpse of the crack closing as if mother earth were finishing her last grunt.

Down I fall for the inner fury of earth. Down I fall hard on the SiO_2 coffin of the emperor's scientifically preserved hard-on.

I have fallen away from NEITHER.

With his fall the empire fell apart like dust after the Richter 8 earthquake which had, after decades' dormancy, rocked the imperial palace like nothing. With his fall fell an unnatural history, his story of faulty campaigns.

Only to be replaced by another erection. Another emperor, another empire. Only slicker and shorter.

Slicker face with unchanging vertical imperial drive. Yet they went on, the cycles, though shorter periods every ensuing come and go, forming an infinite sequence $x_n = b_n u(n)$, $b =$ a fractional, broken down, backwards, u a step function of *ugh ugh*, through the inverse one-sided Z-transform of the ageless divergent absolute power series.

The limit of my patience was tested again and again against the end of the endless line outside the Memorial Hall of the emperor from time immemorial.

A number x is called the limit of a sequence $\{x_n\}$ if for every infinitesimal $\varepsilon > 0$ there exists a natural number $N = N(\varepsilon)$ such that $|x_n - x| < \varepsilon$ for all $n > N$, said Prof. Z.

Did he fall inevitably due to the high potential energy in the imperial palace?

Secret words pound against my breast on the coffin. I must have fallen off ions of He.

Did you fall, where did you fall, he kept asking himself in the hospital bed, fear still in his eyes, in the very room where I had been kept yester-yester-spring, from the fever caught by losing my way in the wind, by losing you and the rest of the party in fighting our way through the crowded mall, through its revolving doors, to the jostling boulevard, on our way to *The Great Escape,* following intoxication in the 3 star restaurant near the Bell Tower in celebration of our 1st Lantern Festival in the ancient city, of our 1st escape from the freshly whitened campus walls, in the chilling fire cracks of the shorter new emperor's 1st campaign to cleanse every wall of words.

The bell rang fearfully.

Did he fear the certainty of the fall or all the odd years to come which were looming larger and larger?

He fell, after an afternoon's card game *Climbing the Ladder*—instead of novels translated from English or in translated English or in original Queen's English or in bastard English, because they had been forbidden again by the Center in the Forbidden City, in the slicker emperor's 2nd campaign to purge *spiritual contamination* —in which he rose step by step faster and faster, in master maneuvers with his new playmate, to the ceiling which is 13 from the bottom rung where she and I looked on helplessly, and then repeated the feat over and over.

He fell as the sun set into an open manhole in the center of the winding path around the manmade lake, while she and I walked on, unaware of his fall until we suddenly realized the huge gap between her left and my right, when we turned around and saw, after scanning left and right up and down, his purple head barely above ground, supported by his stretched arms on the rim of the blind hole, on the rim of his existence.

Even though we were all too familiar with his wayward way of walking, which never followed any given way, always veering right, dragging anyone on his left farther away from the left, and pushing anyone on his right even more to the right. The electromagnetic force would keep the walkers in a straight line segment, normal to the local tangent vector of the however curved way. He never claimed

119

he was a neo-rightist. Neither did he deny his father's life lesson as an ultra-rightist. Until she or he in his right hit or nearly hit another walker, the sidewall, tree, or fast moving bicycle or truck. As we often walked on the main road, which we unanimously preferred to sidewalks for its extra room for lateral movement. And his co-workers had to force him back into the center of the way. But in no time the right drifting would renew its course, as if to test the lateral limit of the way, shrouded by the feeble but unsettling voice *why is the road getting narrower and narrower as life moves on*, thus forming a continuous concatenation of Z, as if a walking meditation about the letter Z in the word *Zeitgeist*, as if a walking homage to Prof. Z.

A function F, defined in the neighbourhood of x_0, has a limit at x_0 iff (if and only if) the right-hand and left-hand limits of F at x_0 both exist and are equal, said Prof. Z.

A function F is continuous at x_0 iff $\lim_{n \to \infty} F(x_n) = F(x_0)$ for all sequences $\{x_n\}$ with F defined in x_n and $\lim_{n \to \infty} x_n = x_0$, said dear Prof. Z.

A function F is continuous at x_0 iff it is continuous from the right and from the left, said dearest Prof. Z.

Did he fall due to exhaustion from prolonged climbing and walking or our centering him again and again?

The bell rings with maddening insistence.

An army of terracotta warriors greets me, reciting *the 1st emperor*, marching in square formations like spectral pixels, bypassing unnamed graves at intersections, where young heads with stainless wounds are half exposed like pimples on the face of the buried city.

Simple graves, simpler hairdos, simplest sentences trapped in-between, simplest music of *1st Piano Concerto* by bursts of netherworld wind, the *Simplex Method* producing no epitaphs no tombstones or anything of that nature, except a few plastic flowers, a few paper spirit moneys.

The war goes on. The war goes on in every martyred facial expression of fear. The war goes on in every pair of lidless bloody eyes of the warriors. The war goes on in every imperative, in every question mark.

It simply happened. An event without answer.

The purple streets form a grid with 4-fold broken rotational symmetry about the axis of the bell tower. It's a blood-baptized conformal (angle-preserving) mapping of the ancient city. All my study about T Square revealed no hint of this underground city. But there has never been any city but this one.

I avoid the warriors, I evade the dead.

For 88 days I ran and ran. I had run 10,000 miles in a giant arc propelled by thin air before my eventual fall. I must have been exported out of Iran 10 millennia ago.

I keep running, through familiar alleys and avenues. Through the unguarded open campus gate, I join you in the old dorm, building 26, room number unclear. You caress the fresh gunshot wound on my buttock.

But I lose you again. Into the pelting purple rain. I jump on my old bicycle to catch up with you, paddle with three legs, blow bullhorn along asphalt road lined with *Firmiana simplex* trees on the deathly empty campus. On and on I race to the ghost beach, assisted by vast horizontal underground movement.

I step into the quiet water as if re-approaching the sentry line. Under the lukewarm sun, the water penetrates my glutei maximi like bayonets.

He blew the bullhorn with the last bit of air in his sinking chest. He blew up the man-made lake in the ancient city and summoned it to the capital. He impressed the ancient square grid of streets onto the center of the lake. He found himself swimming in the moat which, centered at the campanile, circles the fallen capital.

But I am struck by miles-long flotsam: white headbands, red armbands, black armbands, stretches of canvas and newspapers with crying headlines. But not you. I don't see you. I strive to piece together the wrecked *they* for *you*. I strive to pierce the water to locate you. In vain. The water is more viscous than blood than molten steel. I am moored at the outer edge of the moat.

The moat squints at me like an inviting blonde beast. The moat mocks the mantra: *ton shit, ont-hits.*

It was the 1st time in the year he swam and the 1st time ever he swam in the uncharted water in the capital.

I stoop, immerse my entire body, and resurface. 15 repetitions later, the muscles reach thermal equilibrium with the water, as if a temporary agreement had been reached through a decade and a half's truce negotiation. I breaststroke. It is the same old feeling of escaping the ground force. But I want to climb up the other bank.

He touched the slippery surface of the inner bank. Like a Ping-Pong ball ripped by a vicious backhand loop kill by a camouflaged soldier transferred from the sentry post on the boulevard to the moat floor, he rolled down the slope, found himself entangled in the grass at the bottom and was overcome, as if by another blow from a Billy club. *Is this the beginning of the end after all after all that?* After struggling for life with his entire being, he managed to resurface above the water.

You were sitting on the outer bank like rocking lifeboats. He yelled once but the muddy water muffled his voice.

Stroke by stroke word by word I remember each sentence you taught me in the freshman swimming pool.

But he restored his composure. *They are timing your radial lap.* He swallowed the water like holy liquid, steadied his breath like a mud-crowned Zen master, gathered all his strength, which he'd never realized before, and plowed the water with all limbs, like the propeller blades of the human-powered water-bicycle we were so fond of riding in the lake in the ancient city.

I hear you talking, You couldn't even walk in the pool then.

I'd learned to breathe in the hot water of the capital, even with only breaststrokes. Teach me freestyle now.

The moat moans like a river of circular anguish.

On his way back to the outer bank he said to himself, *You have an obligation to speak, are obliged to present your findings to outer space to the entire universe. The effects. And the causes.*

You are walking silently along the outer bank.

I drift circumferentially instead of swimming radially to you. Because you can't swim again in the same moat.

You walked from triangle to square via the 2nd circle. You walked through and through the Square never finding the 1st round hole. You walked from April to June. You walked through an over-determined homogeneous system of linear equations for nontrivial solutions. You walked in a symmetric square matrix. You walked in rows. You walked in columns. You walked in longitudinal waves. You walked in transverse waves. You walked in triangular and square waveforms. You walked in both dilatational and distortional modes. You walked beyond the 1st Brilliant Zone. You walked in detours. You walked in loops. You walked into troops. You walked in different units. You walked in different representations of finite non-Abelian groups. You walked with six flavors. You walked in three colors. You walked alone with yourself, inside yourself, outside yourself. You walked with songs. You walked without words. You walked on stilts. You walked on crutches. You walked like four-legged noncompliant robots. You walked looking neither to the left nor to the right. You walked before sunrise. You walked after curfew. You walked under the fearsome sun. You walked a fine line. You walked on a tight string. You walked away from the center line. You walked without linebreaks. You walked across the lines. You walked carrying loaded integers 7, 12, 2. You walked as if prime stalkers. You walked with snowballing natural numbers. You walked with writing brushes over rice paper, cotton cloth, silk, and satin. You walked when it was raining like shit. You walked when your feet didn't want to. You walked on your heads. You walked headless. You walked naked. You walked undercover. You walked under quotations. You walked under aphorisms, metonymies, acronyms, ideograms, and pictograms. You walked between the lines. You walked with a hard-on between your arms. You walked in hunger. You walked the dehydrated her out of the walking procession to board the subway train. You walked to the subway station to battle the sudden flood of underground army. You walked to bridges and overpasses at the intersections on the 3rd loop to stop armored divisions of the group armies flowing out of the national cemetery. You walked to the bus terminal to find traces of her fluttering hair. You walked way ahead of leading intellectuals who debate in eternity the locomotive mechanisms and intellectual attributes of walking. You walked following the mock coffin from a distance. You walked side by side with toiling doctors. You walked in the midst of fatally unevened even numbers 4, 6, 26. You walked in the shadow of immobile odd numbers -221, 1911, 49, 57, 79, 81, 83, 87. You walked cursing the primeness of 89. You walked with dwindling natural numbers. You walked counting all rational numbers. You walked to chase down every digit after decimal points in the uncountable set of irrational numbers. You walked to the train station only to miss the train to escape. You walked among no strangers. You walked from twilight to limelight to twilight. You walked out of buildings where you're supposed to stay inside. You walked in hallways and corridors when you were prohibited from venturing outside the trembling walls. You walked in the playground to warm up for more serious walking. You walked beside her. You walked after her. You walked looking for her. You walked masturbating emptied bottles in quick successions. You walked when you were not yet ready to walk. You walked along a path never legibly plotted out of the dot matrix printer. You walked when the destination of walking was still up in the air. You walked from east. You walked from west. You walked from north. You walked towards south. You walked to find the direction normal to the plane of the gate. You walked where nobody expected you would have. You walked in εs. You walked through Fast Futurity Transform. You walked in one and the same rhythm as you inhaled and exhaled oxygen. You walked with constant group velocity. You walked to outlast the period. You walked in simple sentences. You walked from subject to object. You walked in grammatically correct order. You walked from Z to A. You walked over discontinuities of the 1st kind. You walked piecewise continuously. You walked as if signifying no other time, no other climate, no other reason, no other degree of freedom. You walked now and now and now. You walked not for the sake of walking. You walked for the namesake of walking. You walked when thinking failed you. You walked because your voice balked at walls of deaf ears. You walked because you were not allowed to talk. You walked when sitting still there was immoral against the morality of sitting in here. You walked because you couldn't stand any longer. You walked in order to demonstrate an order, a long-range order, an order of magnitude of N. You walked since walking was the only means of transportation. You walked since you had been walking for 70 years. You simply walked with no illusion of ending all walking.

You are still walking. 20 millions of you. 10 millions of you. A million of you. 250,000 of you. 100,000 of you.

You are still walking. *{1, 2, 3, 3,000, 300, 20,000, 3, 50,000, 1,000, 12, 100, 100,000, 3,100, 200, 300,000, 1,000,000, 50,000, 1, 1,000, 4, 7,000, 241, 3, 2, 1, . . . }*

Who are you?

I drift amid 319 stained red flags with distinctive names, except the common word *University*. It's such a capital sin of the body not to be able to drown in the ruins.

I hold my breath, I square my questions, real questions such as how well did you know in advance the surface conditions of the Square, how did you prepare yourselves to traverse the Square, how did you arrive at all, by what vehicle, not subways (closed), not buses (appropriated), not electric buses (overturned), not taxicabs (on strike), not motorcycles (banned), no more ambulances (crucified by their own Red Cross signs), never again army trucks (blocked), never again armored vehicles (blocked), never again armed helicopters (scared away by close-up top views of the solemn union of churning masses).

I square and square more questions, imaginary questions like do you still possess your old T-square and your old T Square, is the T Square a blown-up self-adjoint projection of the T-square onto the capital, or the T-square a miniaturized prototype of the T Square.

As if for the Q & A session following my presentation.

I square root, again and again, these complex questions, which boil down to the one and only question, with real part, *what will you miss*, imaginary part, *if you are never able to walk in the T Square again.*

The bell rings and rings.

I drift in the complex conjugate of the ultimate question, that is, *what will you miss if you are able to walk in the T Square again*, circling the inverse square (laws of electricity and gravity).

I look back at the invisible Square.

Will you ever walk again in the T Square or not?

I watched the inverse of the sparse square matrix burn at dawn.

I write Gogo's wife as he says Gilberte *Goddess* the black pages blending blurring banging blazing blaring bleached bluely like the birds scudding away torn by the wind across the flattened sky of the capital because this capital city is capitalized by B being the butcher's face and dressed in the purple bra of bravado of the super-lattice of inertia of impotence strings of atoms of nouns adjectives falling vertically like immortal lines in the ancient Chinese books *interjection daughter dim ambiguous jade*

I write Greek letter as he says Chinese character strings of atoms of verbs adjectives nouns falling obliquely from the south *obstruct detrimental moxa fine old discontinue growth vegetation conceal pass narrow urgent destitute cloudy glasses obscure* subject verb object can we string them together to form a *real* line flakes of October snow fell in closed and open strings beyond superstrings at various incident angles onto scraps of the crumbled marble statue of the *Goddess*

I write winter as he says October yes it's the 1st day of October but the interval bounded by June and winter was null after that because the implosion in the heart of the capital through fission of heavy elements of uranium-like emotions created the instantaneous nuclear winter inside the head by blasting through the silenced channel of the sore blown deep throat a cloud of soot and dust of the disoriented disintegrated feelings which blanketed the tiny planet of the head one layer after another from absorbing any ray of sunlight of revelation and rationalization and reduced its interior temperature of apprehension and expression to -273°C in both its half-spherical chambers

because his radio-cassette player played again and again the one and only melody *New York's Autumn* because the golden autumn is the most beautiful season of the fabled capital because all the gold had been bestowed to and gone with the *Goddess* into the immortal sky because autumn is the season of harvest while the seed of 1st love had been prematurely uprooted and to make the year a nominally constant period of natural time the spring of spring had been doubled and swelled by tears of an idealist's crystalline joy and the amorphous deluge of sorrow and rage of the divergent *geometric* series of *points of views lines of plots polygons of characters* and *circles of references* I write it as he says it

there are no gaps in a *real* line in the 1st spring drizzle in the ancient city he and I confided for the 1st and only time our darkest secrets to each other and vowed they would forever be kept only between us not knowing how to say love because nobody in our life neither our parents nor our teachers nor the late emperor had ever shed on us a single clear light of the manner of saying it in our 1st 15 years' drifting gazing and blundering in the muddy yellow river of small town life

he and I leaned side by side on the wooden arch bridge over the river no kissing or groping or anything like that toward the willow trees on the bank where stand the circularly shaped site of the relics and mummies of the matriarchal clan village to trace any visible signs of our previous lives such as stone axes hoes spades chisels bowls spinning wheels bone needles and fish hooks clay pots portraying fish with open mouths fishnets and doe on the run round and square houses built partly below ground and wooden structures above ground with doors facing south

from where did the deer come how far had she traveled and where is she heading now we were never the same after that after that in the deformed season we were groping for a reason an explanation to the catastrophe yesterday we bicycled again for five hours to the hill to plead the pale maple leaves for an answer to the question *what is real* but more than 5,000 days later they still adamantly refused to appear before us with their true color even the maple trees seemed to have been permanently sickened by the excessive redness of the air empty-handed gazing horizontally at the horizon on the hilltop he asked me why all the words and sentences run horizontally on contemporary pages which blatantly violates the law of gravity there must be another law for the field of the written I write it as he says it

falling colliding and resonating inside the freezing dark room of his skull were fast-growing grains of words *interjection daughter dim ambiguous jade obstruct detrimental moxa fine old discontinue growth vegetation conceal pass narrow urgent destitute cloudy glasses obscure* words which rhyme in Chinese with *love* that is *Ai* and which must not merely rhyme

this rhyme is not accidental these italics are manifestation of the oblique rain this rain never ends this ride has not and will never have an arrival this storm is in the room is the room this room is the black body radiating omnidirectionally at such a temperature that the maximum emission is at the wavelength of yellow this yellow room overlooks and pours into the moaning moat of the capital to find the Gaussian curvature of white heads of the decapitated geese the Green's function and the false projection of the moon

this moon is not realism the image of the man walking on the moon was a total fluke this half dome is a half tome of a heaped looped sentence scribbled by an inchworm on the crowded boulevard in Rome this sentence is a visco-elasto-plastic line this line walks runs pauses leaps turns and breaks grudgingly into multiple lines of even length forced by the hard walls of the page this line is the track left by the sliding and rolling contact of the metal ballpoint on this 8.5×11 black plane of recycled carbonless paper this moving contact is transient thermal history-dependent and irreversible this contact problem rejects closed-form solutions by both Hertz and Love

this linear motion is not linear not driven by syntax or by linear motor this motion distinguishes not night and day because the alternation of black and white has no regular periodicity this line redistributes past and present and future events this line does not belong to any linear space because the rules of associativity of addition and commutativity of addition do not hold because there is not a zero element in it since the subsets of denotations and connotations for any signified or signifier are never null because the rules of distributivity and associativity of multiplication do not apply I write it as he says it

this line is the 1µm thick gold interconnect line the mortal line in the integrated circuit of humane communication which is plagued by growing voids or mass pileup caused by this unprecedented large-scale electro-migration this wind of free electrons this wind of freedom because the design of this accelerated test of reliability of rapid prototyping of blue was intrinsically flawed in its underestimation of the large current density of events and its overestimation of the immobility of atom cores I write it as he says it

this line is not a *real* line because in it gaps abound gaps of irrational shapes of irrational numbers of irrational longings I write *this* as he says *that*

but this longing can not be spelled in any natural language this longing has no metric scheme this longing renounces punctuation

but this feeling is real this feeling is a real-valued function of the unreal time t denoted by F which is disintegrated but still perversely continuous and continuous to the order of ∞ this function spans the entire family of infinitely differentiable real functions in Euclidean space thus supplying the test function for the rigorous definition of the Dirac distribution $\langle \delta, F \rangle = \int_{-\infty}^{\infty} \delta(t) F(t) dt = F(0)$ which is a continuous linear functional that smoothes out the singularity of the δ function and which always assumes the real value of $F(t)$ at origin that is the instant of this once-in-life intimacy with catastrophe yet this function possesses another set of frame of reference with infinite bases which can neither be orthogonized nor normalized in any sense or tense this was is the story he tells me in yesteryear's language at 4:30 AM on the tricycle circling the T Square shoulder to shoulder thigh to thigh butt-welded into one he and I on the back seat by the almost horizontal rain of twilight my left hand in his right hand waiting for the reappearance of that face after this we are one and the same after this we will never be the same again I look at his free or left hand which by thumb and index is holding the yellowish shriveled maple leaf the man on the front seat turns around looking past us soliloquizing *listen 1+1=2 is not the last unproven hypothesis in number theory* the young philosopher now obsessed with the motion of wheel has jumped off the tenure-track to become the egghead cyclist in a circus troupe

at the No. 3002 bus stop at the T Square four dead men are playing *go* while inside the Square among conical dunes of dust a division of identical white butterflies are chorusing *I am a two-month-old china girl and I am the most beautiful of all* and a platoon of baby giant panda are drumming *forest forest bamboo forest Forest of Steles* echoed by murmurs from the featureless gray sky gray from the saturation and hence the disappearance of red through the logic operator NOT and the depletion of green and blue from the massive onslaught by rains of weapons of mass destruction murmurs of mother Green Tara *Om Tare Tuttare Ture Mama Ayuh Punye Gyana Putim Kuru Soha*

there is no point I see no point in further interpretation I smell the last lily of June I usher my lady of flower into my secret glass garden of budding black mushroom I feel an itching in the back of my knees spreading horizontally backwards and vertically downwards at the same time I don't want to go let me go